conversations with Jesus

conversation with Jesus

conversations with Jesus
talk that really matters

REVISED EDITION

Youth For Christ

ZONDERVAN.com/
AUTHORTRACKER
follow your favorite authors

ZONDERVAN

Conversations with Jesus: Talk That Really Matters
Copyright © 2006, 2012 by Youth For Christ

This title is also available as a Zondervan ebook.
Visit www.zondervan.com/ebooks.

Requests for information should be addressed to:

Zondervan, *Grand Rapids, Michigan* 49530

Library of Congress Cataloging-in-Publication Data

Conversations with Jesus : talk that really matters / Youth for Christ. — Rev. ed.
        p. cm.
    ISBN 978-0-310-73004-0 (softcover)
    1. Youth — Prayers and devotions. I. Youth for Christ/USA.
BV4531.3.C66 2011
242'.63 — dc23   2011045491

Cover design: Micah Kandros Design
Interior design: Ben Fetterley & Greg Johnson/Textbook Perfect

Printed in the United States of America

QG 11-01-16

12 13 14 15 16 /QG/ 20 19 18 17 16 15 14 13 12 11 10 9 8 7 6 5 4 3 2

TABLE OF CONTENTS

INTRODUCTION

What Is 3Story®?

3Story is a way of understanding your relationships with God and with other people. Out of a relationship with Christ and others, an amazing, heroic Christian life happens naturally: God's life touches yours and yours touches another's.

Think of three circles representing three stories: God's story, My story, and Their (others') stories. These three circles overlap every day: you and your story with God's story, you and your story with your friend's stories, your friends and their stories with God's story. 3Story is not new; Jesus's life actually characterized this concept. As much as possible, 3Story is a return to a way of living like Jesus did with his disciples. Living out the gospel in actions, not just words.

When you understand how your story affects others' stories, you see how powerful the impact of God's story can be through you. First, let God's story affect yours. Jesus invites you to seek him. To rest in him, and simply be with him. When you do this, your life will show the fruit of God's Spirit—love and self-control, faithfulness and joy—and you will be a pleasure to God and a blessing to others.

Next, pay attention to the stories around you. Discover. Be involved. Ask good questions but also listen. Disclose your story with honesty and realness, sharing who you really are and why you need Jesus. As you are transparent, your story will connect with those stories and with God's.

The more the three stories interact and overlap in your life, the more you'll learn something about yourself, God, and others so you can make important relational connections. And it all starts with the conversations you have with Jesus.

Conversation Guide

This little book is not an ordinary book. It's the result of listening to God speak clearly through his Word and through his Spirit. Are you ready to listen too?

When a group of us from Youth For Christ decided to listen better to the One who speaks quiet words of love, we wondered if it was okay to put those words in writing for others to read. We weren't sure if we'd be offending God by making it look like we thought we could speak for him. (Who can actually speak for God? Only God, right?) After lots of prayer and listening to the Holy Spirit, we decided to take the risk.

The idea of messages that might come from Jesus seems wild, heroic, even scary. When you consider that God Almighty might really want to say something important to you right now, today—WOW! That is freaky and thrilling.

Our group of listeners decided to take the plunge into God's Word and urgently seek him by listening and waiting before putting anything to pen and paper. It wasn't easy. Some of us struggled with spiritual battles and attacks. We felt the weight of listening to God on behalf of others like you.

The idea we pursued was living in Jesus and in his love. We wanted to connect our stories more intimately with God's story. Listening to God is one powerful way of living in Christ so he'll fill our hearts in new ways; his loving conviction will correct us every day; his joy and his sorrow will enable us to receive his love. He will cause his love to overflow from himself to us and then into a broken world where our friends and family members need him as much as we do.

So as you read these devotionals, take time to listen to what God may be saying to you. Read the main Scripture for each devotional, then look up the other Scriptures that go along with it. Ponder the words under "What Jesus Might Say to You"; let them roll around in your mind. Take them in slowly, letting his messages settle into your heart as well. Then jot a few thoughts about how Jesus's words affect your story and how they could affect others' stories. You may be surprised at the new conversations you start having with Jesus—and with those around you.

Acknowledgments

Thanks to the Youth For Christ staff who listen to Jesus and young people every day. And a special thanks to those of you who jotted down what Jesus was saying to you in order to share it in this book.

Devotional 1

you are never alone

TOPIC: Loneliness

MAIN SCRIPTURE: "As I was with Moses, so I will be with you; I will never leave you nor forsake you." (Joshua 1:5)

OTHER SCRIPTURES: Deuteronomy 31:6 – 8; Psalm 23:4; Mark 15:33 – 39; John 14:16 – 19; John 16:4 – 15; Colossians 1:27

WHAT JESUS MIGHT SAY TO YOU: I understand your feelings of loneliness. Your cries in the night, when you feel like no one understands and no one cares, have not gone unheard ... and I do care.

I've known loneliness. While hanging on the cross, I felt the pain of abandonment. In my final moments, I cried out, "My God, my God, why have you forsaken me?" Although he dearly loved me, my Father in heaven couldn't comfort me in my darkest hour, because I was carrying the sins of the world—your sin—on my shoulders, and he couldn't look at the sin. No one before me and no one after me has experienced abandonment and loneliness as deep and painful as that. I understand.

I carried your sin and faced the abandonment of my Father so I could free you from loneliness. Even if you can't see me now, I'm always with you because I live in you. I will never, never leave you nor forsake you. When others fail you or abandon you, I am with you—always.

In moments of desperation, allow your loneliness to drive you closer to me. Don't fill your emptiness with things that can't satisfy. Lean into me—I'm as close as the air you breathe. Cry out to me in pain and remember that I cry out in pain with you.

Devotional 2

give it up

TOPIC: Guilt and Shame

MAIN SCRIPTURES: "So now there is no condemnation for those who belong to Christ Jesus. And because you belong to him, the power of the life-giving Spirit has freed you from the power of sin that leads to death. The law of Moses was unable to save us because of the weakness of our sinful nature. So God did what the law could not do. He sent his own Son in a body like the bodies we sinners have. And in that body God declared an end to sin's control over us by giving his Son as a sacrifice for our sins. He did this so that the just requirement of the law would be fully satisfied for us, who no longer follow our sinful nature but instead follow the Spirit." (Romans 8:1 – 4, NLT)

"Yet now I am happy, not because you were made sorry, but because your sorrow led you to repentance ... Godly sorrow brings repentance that leads to salvation and leaves no regret, but worldly sorrow brings death." (2 Corinthians 7:9 – 10)

OTHER SCRIPTURES: Psalm 103:12; Acts 13:38 – 39; Romans 4:7 – 8; Romans 5:16 – 19; Romans 8:33 – 39; Jude v. 24

WHAT JESUS MIGHT SAY TO YOU: I have something really important to tell you: you don't ever have to feel shame or guilt for the wrong things you've done. Though I want you to recognize your sin and repent from it, I never want it to hold you back. Guilt and shame do not come from me; they work against what I've done for you.

I set you free from sin. Guilt and shame will make you feel unworthy of my love and make you feel as though you have to

You mean more than the world to me, so take this ~~oppor~~tunity to remove yourself from the cares of this world an~~d get~~ closer to the one who will always be with you.

Your faithful friend,

Jesus

HOW JESUS'S WORDS AFFECT MY STORY:

HOW I COULD AFFECT THEIR STORIES:

make up for all the wrong you have done or will ever do again. But let's get something straight; you would never be able to make up for sin. I am too holy; my standards are perfect.

When you sin, my Spirit will convict you about it. You'll know when you've done something wrong. Confess it to me (and to others, especially those who've been affected by your behavior). But then leave it with me, and remember that my sacrifice wipes the slate clean. If you need to make a situation right with another person—through an apology, returning something, or repayment—then do that as soon as possible. But don't dwell on the poor choice, the hurtful behavior, the moral wrong; don't beat yourself up over it. Feeling ongoing guilt or shame is like punishing yourself for the error of your ways, as if punishment could make the wrong go away or cancel it. But I already took the beating for sin. You don't have to. Live freely and forgiven; that's what I want for you.

Not counting sin against you,

Jesus

HOW JESUS'S WORDS AFFECT MY STORY:

HOW I COULD AFFECT THEIR STORIES:

note to self

TOPIC: Identity

MAIN SCRIPTURE: "Though I could have confidence in my own effort if anyone could. Indeed, if others have reason for confidence in their own efforts, I have even more! I was circumcised when I was eight days old. I am a pure-blooded citizen of Israel and a member of the tribe of Benjamin—a real Hebrew if there ever was one! I was a member of the Pharisees, who demand the strictest obedience to the Jewish law. I was so zealous that I harshly persecuted the church. And as for righteousness, I obeyed the law without fault. I once thought these things were valuable, but now I consider them worthless because of what Christ has done ... I no longer count on my own righteousness through obeying the law; rather, I become righteous through faith in Christ. For God's way of making us right with himself depends on faith." (Philippians 3:4–9, NLT)

OTHER SCRIPTURES: Galatians 2:20; Galatians 6:14; 1 John 5:20

WHAT JESUS MIGHT SAY TO YOU: Take note, at your deepest place, at the core of who you are: *You are not a son or a daughter. You are not a sister or a brother. You are not a student or a dropout. You are not smart or not-so-smart. You are not needed or unnecessary. You are not cool or uncool. You are not an original or a slave to fashion. You are not funny or lame. You are not an artist or uncreative. You are not outgoing or shy. You are not popular or a loner. You are not a role model or a rebel.*

These are the masks you may try to hide behind, the places you may run to for shelter, the idols you may bow before. But your identity can't be found in any of these things. You can't become more valuable by building up any of these things. You can't become less valuable by lacking any of these things. You can't be completely fulfilled by relying on or investing in these things.

At your deepest place, at the core of who you are: *You are loved by me. You are simply a naked spirit clothed by my grace. You are my child. You are completely known. You are forgiven. You are brand new. You are precious in my sight. You are held close. You are treasured, and I will never let you go. You are secure, and I will never let you down. You have been chosen to be my friend and coworker. Your heart is my home. You are my beloved. I want you, not the things you hide behind.*

Remember who you really are. Let me be your source of joy, the foundation of your identity, your life.

Your anchor,
Jesus

HOW JESUS'S WORDS AFFECT MY STORY:

HOW I COULD AFFECT THEIR STORIES:

Devotional 4

happiness is overrated

TOPIC: Wholeness

MAIN SCRIPTURES: "Being confident of this, that he who began a good work in you will carry it on to completion until the day of Christ Jesus." (Philippians 1:6)

" 'I've obeyed all these commandments,' the young man replied. 'What else must I do?' Jesus told him, 'If you want to be perfect, go and sell all your possessions and give the money to the poor, and you will have treasure in heaven. Then come, follow me.' " (Matthew 19:20 – 21, NLT)

OTHER SCRIPTURES: John 10:10; Philippians 3:8 – 10; Hebrews 2:10; James 1:4

WHAT JESUS MIGHT SAY TO YOU: How will your life change as a result of knowing me?

Think about the world you live in. It's full of self-consumed people, driven by success and what they think will benefit them. It makes me sad to see how this thinking has corrupted the message of my love. People even try to say that following me will guarantee a happy, easy, problem-free life.

My child, this is not what I have in mind for you. My plan is much bigger. My desires for you are far deeper!

In my letters to you (the Bible) I often use the word *teleios*. In English, this Greek word means "complete, full-grown, becoming the person I created you to be." This is my desire for you: wholeness. I want to heal your heart and enable you to experience the full life I have promised.

Warning: The road to wholeness isn't easy. It's a process. Wholeness doesn't mean problems disappear; it means that because you know me, you lack nothing and are able to weather all of life's storms. In the hard and confusing times remember this: I love you. My heart is unfailing. I'm holding you tight.

Don't ever settle for less than my absolute best for you. The world will try to convince you to take the safe, easy route. Don't cave. I love you far more than you could ever imagine, and I'm preparing you for great things. Trust my love for you. Trust me. I'm worth it.

Holding your heart,

Jesus

HOW JESUS'S WORDS AFFECT MY STORY:

HOW I COULD AFFECT THEIR STORIES:

Devotional 5

in this together

TOPIC: Life in Christ

MAIN SCRIPTURE: "Remain in me, as I also remain in you. No branch can bear fruit by itself; it must remain in the vine. Neither can you bear fruit unless you remain in me. I am the vine; you are the branches. If you remain in me and I in you, you will bear much fruit; apart from me you can do nothing." (John 15:4–5)

OTHER SCRIPTURES: John 15:1–11; Romans 8:11; Galatians 2:20; James 2:17; 1 John 2:24–28

WHAT JESUS MIGHT SAY TO YOU: "Remaining in me" might sound like a sci-fi occurrence, but we are a part of each other. My life is in yours. When you said yes to me, that stuck us together for always. And one of the best parts of that? We get to do amazing things together.

Living in me means getting enough of me so your heart and your mind are strong because of my influence. If you let me direct your life through my own, you'll see how the "fruit" of your life changes for the better. Don't try to go it alone. People will try to tell you that you are king of the hill, queen of the world. They'll say that if you want to do anything good, you better go out there and get after it, take charge, be your own boss, and get it done.

I'm telling you that everything good will come as you walk with me. We'll do this together. Remaining in me is when you let me truly take over. I will transform your mind. I will fill your heart. Letting me envelop your life will result in me becoming a part of who you are. You'll have everything you need for all the battles. When you get tired, I'll give you strength. When you get lonely, I'll be right there with you. And when anyone attacks you, I'll jump in front and take the hits.

Staying in me will also keep you from getting all puffed up and full of yourself. Think about it. Without me, you could strive to be effective by loving and doing good, but no matter how hard you work, it'd be limited. If we do this life together, I'll make a difference in the lives around you, and the work will be easy.

So stay close. Spend time with me. You'll wonder how you ever tried to live with just a little of me. A life full of me is just that—full, with room for nothing else.

The life giver,

Jesus

HOW JESUS'S WORDS AFFECT MY STORY:

HOW I COULD AFFECT THEIR STORIES:

Devotional 6

what's the worry?

TOPIC: Worry

MAIN SCRIPTURE: "Don't worry about anything; instead, pray about everything. Tell God what you need, and thank him for all he has done. Then you will experience God's peace, which exceeds anything we can understand. His peace will guard your hearts and minds as you live in Christ Jesus." (Philippians 4:6–7, NLT)

OTHER SCRIPTURES: Exodus 16:16–21; Matthew 6:25–34; Mark 4:35–41

WHAT JESUS MIGHT SAY TO YOU: Why do you worry and get upset? Have you forgotten how wide and long and high and deep my love is for you? I love you more than life itself. If I can calm the stormiest sea, heal the sick, and raise the dead—if I can overcome death and the grave—then know that my great power far surpasses your greatest problem.

At this very moment the Holy Spirit and I are praying for you to your Father in heaven. We're for you; we're on your side. But best of all, your Father in heaven is for you too. And if God is for you, who can stand against you?

We are praying that you will accept the peace we offer you—peace that's far more wonderful than you can understand, peace that guards your heart and mind as you walk with me. But you need to let go of your worry before you can hold on to my peace.

You don't need to be anxious about tomorrow, because tomorrow will care for itself. Worrying will do nothing to change it. Worrying only fools you into believing that you can change your situation and save yourself. But you can't. I'm the only one who can save you. Don't load yourself up with burdens that don't belong to you. My yoke is easy and my burden is light.

When you struggle with worry, tell me exactly how you feel. Remember, I have taken care of you in the past. Trust that I am in control of your future regardless of what happens right now. Rather than focusing on your problems, focus on me, trusting that I want to solve your problems. Because I do.

Your true peace,
Jesus

HOW JESUS'S WORDS AFFECT MY STORY:

HOW I COULD AFFECT THEIR STORIES:

Devotional 7

risk the relationship

TOPIC: Broken Trust

MAIN SCRIPTURE: "The Lord is my strength and my shield; my heart trusts in him, and he helps me. My heart leaps for joy, and with my song I praise him." (Psalm 28:7)

OTHER SCRIPTURES: Isaiah 26:3; Matthew 11:28; Matthew 26:47–56; Romans 12:21; 2 Timothy 2:13

WHAT JESUS MIGHT SAY TO YOU: Few things hurt as much as trusting someone only to discover that the person can't be trusted. Without trust, a friendship simply does not exist.

I understand your feelings of betrayal, the humiliation of being exposed, and the regret of friendship gone sour. One of my closest followers betrayed me, and it ended up getting me nailed to a cross.

The fact is, no one is completely trustworthy—except me. Others will always let you down, and you will let others down too. In fact, you've let me down at times (you know all about it, so we don't need to get into it), and you will continue to do so in the future. But that doesn't change my undying love for you.

The question is: Where do you go from here?

You can strike back at the person who hurt you, or you can respond in the same way that I always respond to you—with forgiveness and love. Rather than allowing evil to overcome you, overcome evil with good.

You can stay angry, or you can give me your anger. It's okay to tell the person who broke your trust how you feel, but if you take out your anger on that person, you'll probably do or say something you'll later regret. You're better off venting your frustrations on me, because I can handle it.

You can promise yourself that you'll never trust anyone again, or you can risk entering into other trusting relationships. Taking the risk of trusting and being betrayed can be painful, but the alternative—avoiding true relationships altogether—is far worse.

Your trustworthy friend,

Jesus

HOW JESUS'S WORDS AFFECT MY STORY:

HOW I COULD AFFECT THEIR STORIES:

Devotional 8

the next big thing

TOPIC: Materialism

MAIN SCRIPTURE: "I am not saying this because I am in need, for I have learned to be content whatever the circumstances. I know what it is to be in need, and I know what it is to have plenty. I have learned the secret of being content in any and every situation, whether well fed or hungry, whether living in plenty or in want. I can do all this through him who gives me strength." (Philippians 4:11 – 13)

OTHER SCRIPTURES: Deuteronomy 4:24; 1 Kings 3:5 – 14; Proverbs 15:16; Ecclesiastes 5:10 – 12; Matthew 6:19 – 24; 2 Corinthians 8:9; 1 Timothy 6:6 – 10

WHAT JESUS MIGHT SAY TO YOU: I'm jealous. I want your whole heart to myself. Sure, everywhere you look, the next best thing draws your eye: the better phone, laptop, or gadget you can't live without. It's not that phones or laptops are evil; it's the state of your heart I care about. If you think more about the next big thing than you do about my love, it bothers me. Here's why: That stuff will never satisfy. There will always be another thing, another desire, another gotta-have-it item that will call your name. If you're always focused on those things, you will never know the amazing joy that comes from living contentedly in my love. You'll get stuck in that place of wanting, wanting, wanting — and really, who wants to live there?

Go after the things that matter: time with me, wisdom, good relationships. Those things can be upgraded for free, with just a little prayer, time, and energy. The desire for money and stuff will leave you feeling empty. The desire for me, for love and wisdom, will fill you up.

Do you see now why I get jealous? I want what's best for you. And when you keep your eyes on all the things you want (but just can't afford), you'll spend a lot of time feeling unhappy and frustrated. Keep your eyes on me and I'll provide just what you need. The truth is you can't go after all those desires and love me at the same time. You'll have to choose.

Choose me. My love is free.

Far better than the latest gadget,

Jesus

HOW JESUS'S WORDS AFFECT MY STORY:

HOW I COULD AFFECT THEIR STORIES:

Devotional 9

you can do this

TOPIC: Confidence

MAIN SCRIPTURE: "This is my command—be strong and coura-geous! Do not be afraid or discouraged. For the Lord your God is with you wherever you go." (Joshua 1:9, NLT)

OTHER SCRIPTURES: Job 42:1–2; Matthew 25:14–30; Philippians 1:6; Philippians 4:13

WHAT JESUS MIGHT SAY TO YOU: I have big plans for you. You weren't put on this planet to take up space, to occupy a body for seventy years and then pass into oblivion. Oh, no! I planted great-ness in you: seeds of talent, strength, wisdom, and purpose. You are wired to be part of my story on this earth. People are waiting—people who hunger for me, thirst for truth, long for kindness. You can't shrink back. Your loved ones, the people who are watching your life, need you to step up and be who you were created to be—boldly living for me and using your strengths to help others.

It's not as hard as you think. I wired you a certain way. Think about the things I've planted in you—the story of your growing up, your talents, your wisdom, and your compassion for others. Start looking around for ways that you can be my hands and feet—doing the things I would do. Don't worry about messing things up or making mistakes; in fact, I can tell you right now that it won't go perfectly, and that's okay. If you focus on me, messy things won't sideline you, they won't take you out of the game. I am working, and I will use your willing heart to reach people. This is a process, so don't let mistakes or mishaps keep you from being part of my work.

I'll bring you through. I'll make sure that even if you don't do everything perfectly, my plans will still unfold in your life. Be bold. Reach out. Don't be afraid, I am with you every step. There is nothing like being a part of another person's story. Don't let fear rob you of the adventure.

Leading you toward big things,

Jesus

HOW JESUS'S WORDS AFFECT MY STORY:

HOW I COULD AFFECT THEIR STORIES:

Devotional 10

You are not alone

TOPIC: Broken Hearts

MAIN SCRIPTURE: "Whom have I in heaven but you? And earth has nothing I desire besides you. My flesh and my heart may fail, but God is the strength of my heart and my portion forever." (Psalm 73:25 – 26)

OTHER SCRIPTURES: Romans 8:18 – 30; 1 Corinthians 13:4 – 8; Revelation 21:4

WHAT JESUS MIGHT SAY TO YOU: I know your heart hurts sometimes. People can be cruel, bad things happen, and friends sometimes walk away. This world is broken. Ever since sin came into it, things have been falling apart. I came to rescue people from sin, but not everyone said yes to me, so many things are still wrong and painful and broken. One day all those broken things will be fixed, but for now you will have to face some painful things— everyone will.

But you are not alone. I will be right there with you and I will comfort you. I will strengthen you when you get to the end of your rope. Not only that, but I will bring good from every dark place you have to walk through. I know that may not feel like much comfort when the tears come or the pain overwhelms you, but you have to hold on to my truth. I will help you. I will walk with you. That's what love does. You've probably heard how love is patient and kind, trustworthy and protective. My love is all those things, plus it never fails. No matter how deep the hurt or how devastating the wound, my love is like a healing cast that will restore your broken heart.

In the midst of the pain, remember there is more. A day will come when hurt will be a distant memory, betrayals will fade from your mind, and heartbreak will only show up in stories of days long gone. Heaven is real. I will see you there one day, and, gently, I will wipe away every tear.

Your forever companion and friend,

Jesus

HOW JESUS'S WORDS AFFECT MY STORY:

HOW I COULD AFFECT THEIR STORIES:

Devotional 11

the coldness of despair

TOPIC: Encouragement

MAIN SCRIPTURE: "Whom have I in heaven but you? I desire you more than anything on earth. My health may fail, and my spirit may grow weak, but God remains the strength of my heart; he is mine forever." (Psalm 73:25–26, NLT)

OTHER SCRIPTURES: Psalm 42; Proverbs 13:12; Ecclesiastes 4:9–12; Jeremiah 29:11–14; Lamentations 3; Philippians 2:1–4

WHAT JESUS MIGHT SAY TO YOU: We all face different seasons in our lives: Spring, when everything comes to life, and new birth, fresh ideas, and fruitfulness abound. Summer, when everyone is at play, friendships flourish, and hope is fulfilled. Fall, when people are hard at work but also enjoying the fruits of their labors. And winter, when everything seems cold and dead, so rather than venture outdoors, people live by themselves in despair and isolation.

I know that your feelings of discouragement and despair make life miserable for you. But remember that it's only a season. It won't last forever—spring is right around the corner. Also remember that this probably isn't the last winter you will face. More will come, as will more seasons of spring, summer, and fall.

During this cold season of your life, I know you're tempted to avoid venturing outside and feeling the frigid outdoors. It's easier to keep to yourself than to share your pain with someone else. But isolating yourself will do nothing to resolve your despair. If anything, it will only make it worse. This is a good time to seek friends who will encourage you and offer you the warmth of their friendship.

But did you also know that in the cold place where you live, I live too? I am alive and well in every season of your life. Your despair can drive you away from me, or it can lead you toward me, where you will feel the warmth of my friendship. When you seek me with your whole heart, you will find me. I am your hope, your encouragement, and the strength of your heart.

Your encouragement,

Jesus

HOW JESUS'S WORDS AFFECT MY STORY:

HOW I COULD AFFECT THEIR STORIES:

Devotional 12

be who you are

TOPIC: Fear

MAIN SCRIPTURE: "So do not be afraid of them, for there is nothing concealed that will not be disclosed, or hidden that will not be made known. What I tell you in the dark, speak in the daylight; what is whispered in your ear, proclaim from the roofs. Do not be afraid of those who kill the body but cannot kill the soul." (Matthew 10:26–28)

OTHER SCRIPTURES: Psalm 139:14–16; Luke 9:24; Philippians 3:10; 1 John 4:18

WHAT JESUS MIGHT SAY TO YOU: I realize that entering into true relationship is risky. What if people don't like what — or who — they see? Instead of suffering the seemingly unbearable pain of rejection, the easy alternative is to build walls around your heart that no one can penetrate. By acting funny, smart, clueless, sexy, quiet, nice, tough, or whatever, you can keep people away from the real you. Unfortunately, those walls keep me away from you as well.

Don't be afraid of being who you are. I'm crazy about you. I wired you for relationships that go far beyond trivial matters and surface conversations. I created you for intimacy with others ... and with me.

But you can't drink from the cup of relationships without tasting pain. The two go together. When relationships happen, pain happens right in the middle of them. But pain isn't the worst thing that can happen to you. The worst thing that can happen to you is to spend your life with a heart that feels no pain, a heart that is hardened to me and to the people around you.

Only through truly intimate relationships will you experience the satisfaction that comes from being loved for who you are, not what you do. That's how I love you.

So be who you are. Risk relationships. Tear down the walls that keep people from knowing the real you. And remember that I love you just the way you are!

Your Creator,

Jesus

HOW JESUS'S WORDS AFFECT MY STORY:

HOW I COULD AFFECT THEIR STORIES:

Devotional 13

one big happy family

TOPIC: Eternal Life

MAIN SCRIPTURE: "Praise be to the God and Father of our Lord Jesus Christ! In his great mercy he has given us new birth into a living hope through the resurrection of Jesus Christ from the dead." (1 Peter 1:3)

OTHER SCRIPTURES: Romans 5:1 – 2; Romans 8:15; 2 Corinthians 6:17 – 18; Ephesians 1:5

WHAT JESUS MIGHT SAY TO YOU: You and me, we are family. The memories that we create today will last all of eternity. Just think of it: In the same way that you can think back and remember birthday parties and family vacations, you will be able to think back and remember the times that you and I have spent building our relationship, going through difficult times or serving others. And when we see each other face to face, those moments will only get sweeter. We'll be creating memories for the rest of eternity.

I hope that gives you hope for today, knowing that we're just beginning on this ride—that there's so much more ahead for the two of us. I also hope you know that the times you encounter along the journey—all of them—will lead to good things if you keep me first. As we walk through something difficult, you'll get stronger, more courageous, bolder in your faith and wiser for the next trial. As we face things together and you come through on the other side, you'll find out that with me, you are more capable than you ever imagined. You'll have perseverance, character, hope—because you'll have seen me at work and you'll know I can do it again.

Hold on to me. The memories will help you hold on to hope. The hope that being part of my family makes all the difference in this life and the life to come.

Your forever champion and brother,

Jesus

HOW JESUS'S WORDS AFFECT MY STORY:

HOW I COULD AFFECT THEIR STORIES:

Devotional 14

loved from the start

TOPIC: God's Love

MAIN SCRIPTURE: "Furthermore, because we are united with Christ, we have received an inheritance from God, for he chose us in advance, and he makes everything work out according to his plan. God's purpose was that we Jews who were the first to trust in Christ would bring praise and glory to God." (Ephesians 1:11 – 12, NLT)

OTHER SCRIPTURES: Genesis 1:27; Psalm 139:13; 2 Corinthians 2:14; Ephesians 2:4 – 6

WHAT JESUS MIGHT SAY TO YOU: Saying your name makes me smile. Listening to your prayers grips my heart. I love you so much. I'm proud of you. I talk to the Father about you. I keep track of the smallest details of your life. The skeptics say that's impossible. (Their small ideas about me make us all laugh in heaven.) Don't worry. I can handle the weight of the world and much more. No problem.

I have made a place for you here in heaven, a place you can't begin to imagine or comprehend. No words in any language adequately explain it. You will be here with me forever. I am well connected — and now through me, you are too.

I love it when you make other people aware of the reason for your joy and hope. I love to hear you tell your friends that I am your friend. You're worth the exorbitant price I had to pay for your ransom.

Looking forward to all of eternity with you,

Jesus

HOW JESUS'S WORDS AFFECT MY STORY:

HOW I COULD AFFECT THEIR STORIES:

someone in heaven loves you

TOPIC: Broken Hearts

MAIN SCRIPTURE: "Father to the fatherless, defender of widows—this is God, whose dwelling is holy." (Psalm 68:5, NLT)

OTHER SCRIPTURES: Psalm 27:10; Psalm 34:17–18; Psalm 147:3

WHAT JESUS MIGHT SAY TO YOU: Count how many of your friends live with sadness and anger. So many of them come from broken homes without loving fathers.

You've had some tough father moments too. I know it hurts when a father gives no words of love to his children.

Do you see the hurts your friends absorb every week? Their pain grows until it becomes numbness. They need my love. Can you let them know that their heavenly Father loves them?

That's a tough assignment. When an earthly father lets you down, it's easy to get bitter and push everyone away—especially the heavenly Father. When your friends seem hard and angry toward me, show them that my Father's love is real. Listen to their stories. It will probably take awhile to get those stories out, so be patient. They might not have anyone else to turn to. Treat them the way I treated hurting people. They need comfort and encouragement. That's love in action. When the time is right, let them know that your listening ear and your unconditional love come from your heavenly Father. Tell them my heart breaks for them. Tell them my story—I showed up on earth to prove my Father's love. Everywhere I went I told stories about fathers and children so that they (and you) can understand God's unconditional love and forgiveness.

When earthly fathers fail badly, God draws near. He is a Father to the fatherless (as well as to fathers who fail). He provides a new family to those who are lonely and brokenhearted. He hears when you call to him. Try it today. Pour out your heart to him for your friends (and your hurts too). He cares. I care. You'll see.

With the Father's love,

Jesus

HOW JESUS'S WORDS AFFECT MY STORY:

HOW I COULD AFFECT THEIR STORIES:

Devotional 16

under his cover

TOPIC: Righteousness

MAIN SCRIPTURES: "… And be found in him, not having a righteousness of my own that comes from the law, but that which is through faith in Christ—the righteousness that comes from God on the basis of faith." (Philippians 3:9)

"You are the salt of the earth … You are the light of the world. A town built on a hill cannot be hidden." (Matthew 5:13 – 14)

OTHER SCRIPTURES: Genesis 1:27; Genesis 15:6; Psalm 18:20, 24; Romans 3:21 – 22; Romans 10:3 – 4; 2 Corinthians 5:21; Hebrews 10:14

WHAT JESUS MIGHT SAY TO YOU: Trying to be good isn't easy, is it? I know you want to do the right things, but living for me is a lot more than simply trying to be good. It's actually about living the truth that you *are* good. Not because you made your sister's bed or you smiled at that guy when you wanted to punch him in the face; your goodness comes from what I did. When I went to the cross, I took all your sin with me: the bad choices, the dark thoughts, the mean behaviors. I took it all, and, in exchange, I gave you my perfect life—my righteousness.

So now when God looks at you, he sees the beauty of my perfect life wrapped around the unique person we made you to be. Anyone who says yes to me wears that same perfect life. It doesn't matter who you are or where you come from; it doesn't matter what's in your past. When you say yes to me, my righteousness becomes a part of you.

Now that doesn't mean everyone is the same or acts sinlessly—it's not like I've created a bunch of righteous robots. But my righteousness is the same for everyone. It frees you; you no longer carry the weight of paying for your own sin. *I* paid it and set your record straight in God's eyes.

Trust that I paid a huge price to bring righteousness to you. You are mine. Made in my image. Live that out this very day.

Proud that you're looking more like me every day,

Jesus

HOW JESUS'S WORDS AFFECT MY STORY:

HOW I COULD AFFECT THEIR STORIES:

Devotional 17

no junk

TOPIC: Self-Image

MAIN SCRIPTURE: "For once you were full of darkness, but now you have light from the Lord. So live as people of light!" (Ephesians 5:8, NLT)

OTHER SCRIPTURES: John 10:7 – 15; Romans 12:1 – 2; 2 Corinthians 5:17; 1 Peter 2:9

WHAT JESUS MIGHT SAY TO YOU: You're not junk. Not even close.

I'm angry when I hear the Enemy, Satan, telling you outright lies about who you are. He's the father of all liars. He's all about stealing hope, killing, and destroying people. He uses people who talk trash to you and put you down. He rejoices when the culture of celebrity brainwashes you into thinking you're not beautiful enough or cool enough. They're all lies.

Let me help you flush out all the poisonous lies you've believed about yourself. Your true value isn't defined or measured by physical beauty or your ability to achieve some big goal or entertain others. Let go of those lies. Focus on being alive and growing in me today. Find your real worth and purpose as a priceless child of God the Father. No one and nothing can ever take that away from you.

When that dark cloud of feeling dumb, ugly, or unloved hangs over your head, let me whisper the truth in your ear—you are a new creation with me in your life. The old is gone. Your past is forgiven and forgotten.

Abide with me today. Meditate on my Word and let it reprogram your mind. Listen to my voice. Believe the truth about who you are in me.

Telling you the truth,

Jesus

HOW JESUS'S WORDS AFFECT MY STORY:

HOW I COULD AFFECT THEIR STORIES:

Devotional 18

more, more, more?

TOPIC: Contentment

MAIN SCRIPTURE: "For I have learned how to be content with whatever I have. I know how to live on almost nothing or with everything. I have learned the secret of living in every situation, whether it is with a full stomach or empty, with plenty or little. For I can do everything through Christ, who gives me strength." (Philippians 4:11 – 13, NLT)

OTHER SCRIPTURES: Matthew 6:24 – 34; Luke 12:15 – 21; 1 Timothy 6:10; Philippians 4:12 – 13

WHAT JESUS MIGHT SAY TO YOU: How much time do you spend thinking about your stuff? When you wake up in the morning, you may worry about what you are going to wear and what kind of an impression it will make. During the day you may wonder when you'll have enough money to get the newest pair of shoes or that brand-name shirt you've been eyeing. And holidays? Those are the worst. How many hours are spent occupying your mind with what you want to put on your birthday or Christmas list? That's a lot of wasted time. None of that stuff is yours anyway. It's all mine.

Why worry? I give you what you need and sometimes what you want. I give to you from my goodness, sometimes to bless you, other times to give you a tool for a greater purpose. So doesn't it seem a bit silly to get wrapped up in thinking about what else you want or think you need? I will take care of those things. If you learn this concept now, then as you get older you'll trust me to provide for your needs and learn to be content with what you have. If you don't learn this today, you may set yourself up to fall into the trap of materialism, always wanting more and more and more.

Think about the ads for cell phones or apps—every few months, there's a new version. So how long could you possibly be satisfied with the last version? It will be outdated in such a short time. What a vicious cycle—the new becomes old and you feel left behind all over again—until you get the new. Getting more stuff doesn't meet your real needs—but it does feed discontent. Instead, hunger for me and what I can give you. Instead, put me first. Find your happiness and fulfillment in me. I know what you need and want and, trust me, I want the best for you.

More satisfying than anything,

Jesus

HOW JESUS'S WORDS AFFECT MY STORY:

HOW I COULD AFFECT THEIR STORIES:

live freely

TOPIC: Peer Pressure

MAIN SCRIPTURE: "There is no fear in love. But perfect love drives out fear, because fear has to do with punishment. The one who fears is not made perfect in love." (1 John 4:18)

OTHER SCRIPTURES: Matthew 26:69–75; John 18:25–27; Romans 1:16; 2 Timothy 1:8

WHAT JESUS MIGHT SAY TO YOU: Don't be afraid. I've been saying that to all of my disciples since I was here on the earth. Don't be afraid of what others think or say about you. They don't know you like I do. Don't let their opinions define who you are. My unconditional love gives you freedom to be the real you—the you I created.

That inner pressure that pushes you to do stupid, wrong, or hurtful things so other people will like you—I know that's not the real you. That junk comes from old insecurities and fears. You and I need to be connected today. I want to see the real you come alive. Be confident of my presence in your life today. My death on the cross is proof that I love you. Don't be afraid.

My disciple Peter told me peer pressure would never bother him. He bragged that he would be with me all the way even if it cost him his life. I knew better. I told him he would find out the truth about himself that same night. Did you hear what happened to him? Three times that night he denied he even knew me. The last time was to a young girl who was no threat at all to him. That broke him.

The next time I saw him, I asked him if he loved me. That's all that really mattered. It shook him up when he understood that I was never going to reject him. From that point on he started living like knowing me and obeying me was more important than his reputation with his buddies. That freed him to be the real Peter and do awesome things for me and the people around him.

That's the same connection I want with you today. Even better—when your friends see the real you living freely, with my constant love inside you, they will want to know your secret. Be ready to reveal it to them.

Live free,

Jesus

HOW JESUS'S WORDS AFFECT MY STORY:

HOW I COULD AFFECT THEIR STORIES:

Devotional 20

what becomes of the brokenhearted?

TOPIC: Broken Hearts

MAIN SCRIPTURE: "The LORD observed the extent of human wickedness on the earth, and he saw that everything they thought or imagined was consistently and totally evil. So the LORD was sorry he had ever made them and put them on the earth. It broke his heart." (Genesis 6:5–6, NLT)

OTHER SCRIPTURES: Psalm 30:2–3, 11–12; Psalm 34:18; Isaiah 53:3; Jeremiah 31:13; Luke 7:12–14

WHAT JESUS MIGHT SAY TO YOU: Few things hurt worse than a broken heart. It feels like the end of the world. Your heart is the core of who you are. When it feels out of order, so does everything else.

Did you read my words in Genesis 6? You're not alone. My heart absolutely breaks when people turn from me and reject my love. Know that when you are hurting, I understand and am there with you. Invite me into your pain. Rest in my unchanging love for you as I carry you down the road of healing. But what does this road look like? How do we survive and move on?

In Isaiah I'm described as a man of sorrows, but I wasn't a sad man. How am I filled with joy, peace, love, and hope while suffering a broken heart? Because my Father's love sustains me.

A broken heart is not easily fixed. You may be tempted to lock up your heart and throw away the key, to protect your heart and never love again. It may seem safer, but it will only cause more pain. If you cease to love, your heart will die. Your heart was created to love because I made it. I am love. You can't truly love and experience the life I intend for you if you ignore your heart to avoid hurt. This is why I don't protect my heart from brokenness. The answer is always more love, not less. Be brokenhearted, not hard-hearted!

To live a life of love means risking a broken heart. Keep loving. Trust in me. Let me be your joy and strength. This is the way to healing. You will make it and it will be worth it.

Holding you close,
Jesus

HOW JESUS'S WORDS AFFECT MY STORY:

HOW I COULD AFFECT THEIR STORIES:

Devotional 21

unlikely heroes

TOPIC: Weakness

MAIN SCRIPTURE: "In the same way, was not even Rahab the prostitute considered righteous for what she did when she gave lodging to the spies and sent them off in a different direction?" (James 2:25)

OTHER SCRIPTURES: Joshua 2; Joshua 6:17; Matthew 5:3–10; 1 Corinthians 1:27

WHAT JESUS MIGHT SAY TO YOU: Today I want to talk about your feelings of inadequacy. It's a lie that you're not good enough to follow me or represent me to the world. I know the world prizes the strong and successful. My way is different. I look for those with humble hearts, aware of their weaknesses. Those who give me room to work in them and through them. These are the people I want to use. Have you read the story of my servant Rahab in Joshua 2? Go ahead. Read it.

I chose to use Rahab in a mighty way. Why? Was it because she was popular and well-respected? No, quite the opposite. In fact, Rahab was a prostitute. But I chose her. And not only did she change the world, but she also had a profound experience of my grace and mercy in the process.

Fast-forward a few years. Rahab had a son named Boaz. Boaz is considered one of the greatest examples of grace and mercy in history. (Check out the book of Ruth.) How did Boaz learn to be so godly and merciful? It was from his mother, the former prostitute.

Remember David—the humble shepherd boy who became a great king, a king after my own heart? He was also a descendant of Rahab and Boaz. Furthermore, guess who else descended from Rahab? I did.

I would rather change the world through a humble prostitute or shepherd boy than through a prideful, religious person who thinks he has it all together. I can't use those who think they have no need for me.

Are you imperfect? Messed up? Do you need me? If the answer is yes, you're in good shape. I can use you. I want to use you to change the world ... and I will.

Going against the flow,

Jesus

HOW JESUS'S WORDS AFFECT MY STORY:

HOW I COULD AFFECT THEIR STORIES:

Devotional 22

the greatest power

TOPIC: Love

MAIN SCRIPTURE: "Three things will last forever—faith, hope, and love—and the greatest of these is love." (1 Corinthians 13:13, NLT)

OTHER SCRIPTURES: John 13:34–35; 1 Thessalonians 3:12–13; 1 John 4:10–12

WHAT JESUS MIGHT SAY TO YOU: I'm crazy about love. Not just the love you and I share, but the love that makes an everyday difference in the lives around you. You need the people around you, and they need you too. Your parents, brothers, sisters, friends, and everyone you love needs to know that they matter to you.

Don't hold back. Love with all you've got. Then ask me to help you love the same way that I have loved you. I don't weigh out whether you "deserve" my love every day. I just love you. Period.

Do the same with the people around you. I gave my life. You give your life by sharing all you are. You have nothing to lose. Yes, it will hurt when people reject your love. I know all about that. But the reward when it all comes together totally outweighs the pain when it doesn't.

I don't want you to love just your family and close friends either. I want you to love your neighbors, the homeless, the hurting. It's easy to think that to stay safe and happy, you should close up and hole up. I tell you the exact opposite is true—because I have lived it myself. I gave it all and I don't regret it for a minute. Love. Serve. Show people the way I love by loving with the same kind of wild abandon. It won't be easy, but I will make it possible for you to love people well, even those who are hard to love.

One last thing. I put my life on the line for love. So while words are good, make sure that your love takes action. Clean up the neighbor's lawn, help a single mom with her kids, bring a meal to someone who is sick.

When people see how you love, they'll get a glimpse of me.

Loving you and loving others,

Jesus

HOW JESUS'S WORDS AFFECT MY STORY:

HOW I COULD AFFECT THEIR STORIES:

Devotional 23

God speaks through you

TOPIC: Sharing Faith

MAIN SCRIPTURE: "So we are Christ's ambassadors; God is making his appeal through us. We speak for Christ when we plead, 'Come back to God!'" (2 Corinthians 5:20, NLT)

OTHER SCRIPTURES: 1 Corinthians 2:1–5; 2 Corinthians 2:16; Ephesians 6:19

WHAT JESUS MIGHT SAY TO YOU: I know this is important for us to talk about. Sometimes this is difficult for some people who love me. They don't want to look like they're pressuring people or selling religion.

Some people want me to light up the sky and do flashy miracles, thinking that will cause everyone to believe in me. I could do it. But most often that's not God's plan. His plan is simple. He sent me to you, and I send you to others. Share my story person to person, life to life. You're a walking, talking example of me living in you.

Remember—it's not about you. No sales quotas or high pressure. I'm the one who lived the sinless life, died on the cross for the sins of the world, and defeated death. Keep the focus on my life, death, and resurrection. Avoid pointless arguments that go nowhere. Let them know you didn't deserve or earn grace and forgiveness. They are gifts from a loving God. Invite them to connect their lives with me as you did.

Keep it simple. Keep it real. The world is overloaded with crazy ideas that try to explain the meaning of life. When you tell my story using words others can understand, and they see authentic changes in your life, I will become real to them.

Not everyone will like you or your message. Some people will hate you (and me) when you talk about the good news. It can be discouraging. Keep on loving these people. Pray for them. God loves them as much he loves you!

But to the people who are seeking God, your life and message will be like the aroma of a delicious meal or the most wonderful perfume. Let me work through your life to reach your friends.

Love,

Jesus

HOW JESUS'S WORDS AFFECT MY STORY:

HOW I COULD AFFECT THEIR STORIES:

Devotional 24

after life here ends

TOPIC: Heaven

MAIN SCRIPTURE: "I have told you these things so that you will be filled with my joy. Yes, your joy will overflow!" (John 15:11, NLT)

OTHER SCRIPTURES: Luke 10:20; Romans 14:7; 1 Peter 1:8

WHAT JESUS MIGHT SAY TO YOU: When you said yes to me, your name was scribed in big bold letters into *the* Book. This is a lot bigger than the Who's Who of high school students or being inducted into the sports hall of fame. It's more exciting than a backstage pass to meet your favorite band or the VIP treatment at the White House. Because your name is written in the Book of Life, you have access to all that you need here on earth: my love, strength, wisdom, truth, and passion. On top of that, you have entrance into heaven. Heaven! Gold streets, wild adventures, unending joy, and friendships that will never be damaged by betrayal or anger or stupid mistakes.

This is big. The joy of knowing your name is forever inscribed should fill you up with joy today. That kind of future should give you boldness to live for me every moment. It will help you obey me, stand with me, tell others all about me. If you let that joy sink deep into your soul, then nothing here on earth will be able to rip it away from you. Sure, you still have to live on earth, which will bring tough times, tears, or anger, but underneath all of that can be a foundation of joy, because you know what lies ahead. This life isn't the end.

I died on a cross for the joy that was right around the corner. I knew that I would see my Father soon. I knew that I was doing something that would bring you to him and me. You'll get to be with me soon.

There is no greater joy.

Waiting to see you,

Jesus

HOW JESUS'S WORDS AFFECT MY STORY:

HOW I COULD AFFECT THEIR STORIES:

afraid of nothing

TOPIC: Fear

MAIN SCRIPTURES: "When I am afraid, I put my trust in you." (Psalm 56:3)

"In my distress I prayed to the LORD, and the LORD answered me and set me free. The LORD is for me, so I will have no fear. What can mere people do to me? Yes, the LORD is for me; he will help me. I will look in triumph at those who hate me." (Psalm 118:5–7, NLT)

OTHER SCRIPTURES: Deuteronomy 3:21–22; Psalm 40:3–4; Isaiah 43:1–3; Philippians 4:6–7

WHAT JESUS MIGHT SAY TO YOU: Everyone feels fear sometimes. My prophet Elijah was terrified of his wicked queen even though I'd just sent fire from the sky to prove myself to some false prophets. King David was afraid at times, and he was known as one of the greatest and strongest kings of Israel. My disciples, who spent every day with me, had their moments too. But I reminded all of them that they did not have to be afraid. I am stronger. I am greater. I am more powerful than anything you will face.

Peers may make fun of you. Some may threaten you or try to push you down. Others may attack your beliefs. Your family may fall apart. But you know what? None of these things are out of my control. Don't let them scare you. Even scary or out-of-control situations are part of my world, my plan. I've got your back. I may not let you see how I'm working, but trust me, I'm always working. I will care for you. When it feels like everything around you is in upheaval, remember that you serve me. I am powerful and mighty, your awesome God who will not let anything get by without going through my hands first.

So much is going on in the world, but I orchestrate it all for my plans and purposes. Have you read about Gideon? He was what you might call a wimpy guy. He was scared of the enemies around his country; he was scared to go into battle; he was scared to trust me. But once he did, I put him in charge of a small army that beat the enemies to pieces. Then I turned him into a leader of his country. When you look around you, it's easy to feel afraid. But when you look at me and keep your focus there, you have no reason to fear.

No fear,

Jesus

HOW JESUS'S WORDS AFFECT MY STORY:

HOW I COULD AFFECT THEIR STORIES:

Devotional 26

this is not your home

TOPIC: Hard Times

MAIN SCRIPTURE: "Restore our fortunes, Lord, as streams renew the desert. Those who plant in tears will harvest with shouts of joy. They weep as they go to plant their seed, but they sing as they return with the harvest." (Psalm 126:4 – 6, NLT)

OTHER SCRIPTURES: Jeremiah 29:11 – 14; John 14:27; 2 Corinthians 4:7 – 9

WHAT JESUS MIGHT SAY TO YOU: This is not your home. At creation, I intended people to live in a world without sin, in a place of joy, life, and love. When sin came into the picture, the whole world changed. Sin separated people from me. Evil started taking over, and things got messy for everyone. So now you're like a fish out of water and you have to learn to live on dry land, which is challenging, to say the least. It's not easy, but you can do it and I will help you. You just have to remember who you are, and live knowing that one day you'll go to your true home.

Many of the good things I created are still on earth, but hard times will come. Pain will be part of this life. You may have to push through difficult circumstances or fight feelings of sadness, disappointment, or despair. Tears may come, and you may be tempted to hide out. Don't. Don't shrink back. I want you to live. Be a part of this world by working with me to rescue the broken and still enjoy all that is good. Tell others of a home that can be theirs as well.

When you do that, reach beyond yourself when you face hard times and bring a touch of home to this land. Then wait expectantly for me to come back for you. I'm coming soon, so hold on.

Knowing it will be worth it in the end,

Jesus

HOW JESUS'S WORDS AFFECT MY STORY:

HOW I COULD AFFECT THEIR STORIES:

overcoming the beast within

TOPIC: Lust

MAIN SCRIPTURE: "Those who live according to the flesh have their minds set on what the flesh desires; but those who live in accordance with the Spirit have their minds set on what the Spirit desires." (Romans 8:5)

OTHER SCRIPTURES: Job 31:1; Proverbs 6:20–29; John 14:6; Romans 6–7; 1 Thessalonians 4:3–8; James 1:14–15; 1 Peter 2:11

WHAT JESUS MIGHT SAY TO YOU: I know you ask yourself, "How can I ever overcome this enormous preoccupation with sex?" I also know that you ask yourself, "What's wrong with sex, anyway?" Sometimes it feels like a battle is being waged.

Right now I know that your hormones are raging, sexual images are assaulting you, and the pressure is increasing, like some animal inside you just pacing its cage.

But would you be surprised to know that I created you with that appetite? Sex is good. It's supposed to be really good. But it's not just some bodily function. It's part of my plan for your happiness. You were designed for the pleasure and fulfillment that comes within the intimate relationship of a man and a woman who are committed to one another for life.

In the meantime the animal inside you needs to remain in its cage. Allowing your sex drive to run free will only get you in trouble and drive you away from me. The battle to bring it under control begins with the influences around you. The TV shows and movies you watch and the music you listen to can feed the animal inside until it seems like it's going crazy, trying to break free from its cage. TV shows, movies, and music don't represent a realistic view of sex, anyway. You've been created as a sexual being, but remember: you are *more* than just a sexual being.

You become what you behold. In other words, if you focus your mind on sex, then sex will become the greatest focus (and obstacle) in your life. If you focus your mind solely on trying to overcome your lust, then sex will still be the focus (and greatest obstacle) in your life. But if you focus on me, you will become like me, and the beast won't be in control.

So run from temptation. Get rid of any influence that feeds the beast inside. And rather than indulging yourself in sex or obsessing on overcoming your problem with lust, indulge yourself in me. I know what you're going through.

Your Creator,

Jesus

HOW JESUS'S WORDS AFFECT MY STORY:

HOW I COULD AFFECT THEIR STORIES:

Devotional 28

talking is overrated

TOPIC: Friendship

MAIN SCRIPTURE: "When Job's three friends, Eliphaz the Temanite, Bildad the Shuhite and Zophar the Naamathite, heard about all the troubles that had come upon him, they set out from their homes and met together by agreement to go and sympathize with him and comfort him. When they saw him from a distance, they could hardly recognize him; they began to weep aloud, and they tore their robes and sprinkled dust on their heads. Then they sat on the ground with him for seven days and seven nights. No one said a word to him, because they saw how great his suffering was." (Job 2:11 – 13)

OTHER SCRIPTURES: Job 13:4 – 5; Proverbs 17:27 – 28; 2 Corinthians 1:4

WHAT JESUS MIGHT SAY TO YOU: My Father is a wonderful listener. During my time here on earth, I would head out into the woods or up into the mountains to spend time with him. Things would get overwhelming; the crowds would begin to push in, and I had to take time to talk and get things off my mind and heart.

You need that too, and so do your friends. If you have a friend who is going through a rough time, the best thing you can do is listen. It's easy to try to fix it, to give your friend advice and point him in a helpful direction, but be careful. First, listen. Then listen some more. You don't have to fix it; that's what I'm here for. You just need to be around — be available.

Another lousy thing to do is beat down a friend when she just needs you to hear her. You know what I'm talking about.

She comes to you to tell you she messed up so you jump in and remind her how bad she was. Sometimes friends do that to each other; and often it does nothing but make things worse.

Here's the truth for you and your friends: Point each other to me. Remind one another that I'm here and I won't let you down. Pray for one another, and be a good listener. Listening says, "You matter to me. I want to hear what's on your mind and in your heart."

That's what I say to you. That's what you can say to your friends.

Always listening,

Jesus

HOW JESUS'S WORDS AFFECT MY STORY:

HOW I COULD AFFECT THEIR STORIES:

Devotional 29

bending the rules

TOPIC: Heart Matters

MAIN SCRIPTURES: "Make a tree good and its fruit will be good, or make a tree bad and its fruit will be bad, for a tree is recognized by its fruit. You brood of vipers, how can you who are evil say anything good? For the mouth speaks what the heart is full of. A good man brings good things out of the good stored up in him, and an evil man brings evil things out of the evil stored up in him." (Matthew 12:33–35)

"If you declare with your mouth, "Jesus is Lord," and believe in your heart that God raised him from the dead, you will be saved. For it is with your heart that you believe and are justified, and it is with your mouth that you profess your faith and are saved." (Romans 10:9–10)

OTHER SCRIPTURES: Matthew 15:18–19; Mark 12:30–33; John 8:3–11

WHAT JESUS MIGHT SAY TO YOU: Some Christians today believe that fixing a non-Christian's morals and behavior is the first step in introducing them to me. Not true! This leads to a dangerous "us versus them" mentality. Many of my followers believe that their morality makes them superior to the world. Sounds a lot like the Pharisees, doesn't it?

This is not my way. The last thing people want to hear is how you think they should act or think. People don't respond positively to this, and besides, morals don't save you. My Word says that a person's actions reveal her heart. The heart is where problems reside. Poor choices are merely symptoms. You don't heal the flu by stopping a sneeze.

Changed behavior is the result of a changed heart. Rules don't change hearts. Only love changes hearts. This is my way. This is what I died for.

If you want someone to know me truly, my love must be your motive and your message. Focus on the internal, not the external. Rather than condemning them, listen to them. Understand their hearts and where they're coming from. Focus on their needs and their desires in light of my grace, my forgiveness, and my unconditional love.

I'll meet them exactly where they are. I am what their hearts have been searching for. When they find fulfillment in me, they'll stop seeking it elsewhere. Their choices will change. Because the concepts of right and wrong don't motivate change. Judgment certainly doesn't motivate change. Relationships motivate change. Love motivates change. This is my message. I am *for* people, not against them.

My message is simple: love me and love others. When you do, you will see the world change ... one life at a time.

My love is greater than any law,

Jesus

HOW JESUS'S WORDS AFFECT MY STORY:

HOW I COULD AFFECT THEIR STORIES:

Devotional 30

Your reservations are confirmed

TOPIC: Fear of Death

MAIN SCRIPTURES: "For to me, living means living for Christ, and dying is even better." (Philippians 1:21, NLT)

"For God so loved the world that he gave his one and only Son, that whoever believes in him shall not perish but have eternal life." (John 3:16)

OTHER SCRIPTURES: John 14:1–6; 1 Corinthians 15:12–23; Philippians 1:21–24

WHAT JESUS MIGHT SAY TO YOU: Tell me what scares you about death. It terrifies most people who talk to me. In fact, when death is nearby, people start talking to me like crazy. People I haven't heard from in years immediately want my attention.

You know my story, right? I was killed when I lived in my human body on earth. It wasn't pretty. I died a horrible death and experienced unbelievable pain. The worst part was the separation from God (my Father) that I experienced when I took on the sin of the whole world (yours included). I was still me. I had absolute power that day. At any point I could've turned away from that horror, but I went the whole way to break death's hold on you so you wouldn't have to be afraid of death. I did what no other "religious leader" ever did. I died and came back to life—and I'm still alive. I'm talking to you every day through the Holy Spirit.

Thomas, my famous doubting disciple, was scared about being separated from me when I died. I told him I was going ahead to prepare a place for him (and you). That place is real and waiting for you when your life on earth is over. Thomas even wanted directions on how to get there. I told him (and you too) that I am the way, the truth, and the life (John 14:6). No one can come to God the Father except through me. Put your faith and trust in me, and you secure a place with me in heaven forever. It's all paid for by my death and guaranteed by my resurrection. So when you die, you have no reason to be afraid.

When your friends talk about death, let them know I've shown you the way to heaven. Tell them my story. They have nothing to fear.

Waiting for you,
Jesus

HOW JESUS'S WORDS AFFECT MY STORY:

HOW I COULD AFFECT THEIR STORIES:

get out of your comfort zone

TOPIC: Boldness

MAIN SCRIPTURES: "But how can they call on him to save them unless they believe in him? And how can they believe in him if they have never heard about him? And how can they hear about him unless someone tells them? And how will anyone go and tell them without being sent? That is why the Scriptures say, 'How beautiful are the feet of messengers who bring good news!'" (Romans 10:14 – 15, NLT)

"We proclaim Him, admonishing every man and teaching every man with all wisdom, so that we may present every man complete in Christ. For this purpose also I labor, striving according to His power, which mightily works within me." (Colossians 1:28 – 29, NASB)

OTHER SCRIPTURES: Jeremiah 20:9; Mark 16:15; John 17:16, 18; Colossians 1:28 – 29; Colossians 4:5 – 7; 1 John 3:18

WHAT JESUS MIGHT SAY TO YOU: I talk about you all the time because you are important to me. I tell my Father about you and ask him to help you, strengthen you, give you what you need to make it in this life.

I want you to talk about me too. I don't want you to make things up or try to sound spiritual; I just want you to tell your friends about who I am in your life. Tell them about moments when I've helped you or times when you have felt my presence in a special way. Your friends need me too. And while they can go to church and hear all about me from a pastor or teacher, it makes a bigger impact when you talk about your experience with me. It's like the difference between watching a commercial for a great movie and hearing from a friend how wonderful it really was. You're much more likely to believe your friends.

My greatest hope is that you won't be able to contain your love for me. I want you to feel so tuned in to my love, so aware of my presence, that you can't help but talk about me to everyone you meet. Think of other people you love or admire. You talk openly and joyfully about them — your best friend, a favorite aunt, a great coach, a fun teacher. You want others to know about those people.

Draw so close to me that it feels natural and good to talk about me. Then others will sense your joy and the reality of your words, and they will want what you have. That's what it means to draw people to me. Not as hard as you imagined, is it?

Worth talking about,

Jesus

HOW JESUS'S WORDS AFFECT MY STORY:

HOW I COULD AFFECT THEIR STORIES:

Devotional 32

does the pain go away?

TOPIC: Loss

MAIN SCRIPTURE: "But he said to me, 'My grace is sufficient for you, for my power is made perfect in weakness.' Therefore I will boast all the more gladly about my weaknesses, so that Christ's power may rest on me." (2 Corinthians 12:9)

OTHER SCRIPTURES: 2 Samuel 22:32–34; Psalm 61:1–4; Psalm 62:1–2; Matthew 27:45–46; Mark 15:34; Acts 14:21–23

WHAT JESUS MIGHT SAY TO YOU: I know what it's like. I know what it feels like to have your whole world fall apart. I understand when it seems like no one is listening and no one cares. When I was on the earth, I went through a lot of painful times. I didn't have a home to call my own, people kept trying to capture and kill me, and then a close friend betrayed me and handed me over to my enemies. I never felt so alone as when I breathed my last few breaths on that cross. I was beaten and bruised and dying, and I cried out to my Father to ask why he had forgotten me.

So you are not alone. When it feels like no one is there, I know better than anyone what that feels like. Oh, how I want to comfort you; know you have a safe place to run. When life feels overwhelming, when you've been rejected and betrayed, I will be your strong protector. I will be your strong tower. I will be your fortress. Just like God heard my cry on the cross, and moments later I was in his presence—so it is with me. Call out to me. I will hear your cry, and I will come to you. I will bring my comfort, my strength, and my love—you'll be able to find safety under my wing. Before you run to your best friend, before you vent in your journal, come to me. Talk to me and know that I'm listening.

Always here whenever you need me,

Jesus

HOW JESUS'S WORDS AFFECT MY STORY:

HOW I COULD AFFECT THEIR STORIES:

Devotional 33

the opposition

TOPIC: The Enemy's Schemes

MAIN SCRIPTURES: "Be alert and of sober mind. Your enemy the devil prowls around like a roaring lion looking for someone to devour. Resist him, standing firm in the faith, because you know that the family of believers throughout the world is undergoing the same kind of sufferings." (1 Peter 5:8–9)

"He was a murderer from the beginning. He has always hated the truth, because there is no truth in him. When he lies, it is consistent with his character; for he is a liar and the father of lies." (John 8:44, NLT)

OTHER SCRIPTURES: Psalm 143:3–4; John 10:10; Acts 10:38; 2 Corinthians 2:11; 2 Corinthians 11:14; 1 John 3:8; Revelation 12:17

WHAT JESUS MIGHT SAY TO YOU: Satan will press you ... he knows exactly which buttons to push. He'll do anything to keep you from all that is worthy of your attention. He will attack your heart, the core of who you are. If anything is good or beautiful or life-giving, he'll try to take it from you. Why? Because he's afraid of you. He knows exactly who I have created you to be. You're a threat to him!

Please understand how Satan works. His schemes may seem complex and twisted, but they're actually quite childish and simple. He is just waving his arms around, shouting, "Look over here!" to distract you, scare you, and get you to take your eyes off me. He'll do anything to keep you from the unfathomable love and great adventure I have for you.

He knows your weaknesses and insecurities. Does this sound familiar? "I can't do that because ..." or "I'm terrible at this ..." or "They're trying to hurt my feelings ..." or "I'm not good enough," etc.? Do NOT listen or agree! That's Satan! He strikes at the very core of your emotions, your insecurities, your identity.

Never respond by giving him your time or attention. Recognize the lies. Turn your eyes back to me. Remember who you are, who I made you to be. Don't let him fool you. I will help you fight! We have already won the war. We can take him.

Your Defender,
Jesus

HOW JESUS'S WORDS AFFECT MY STORY:

HOW I COULD AFFECT THEIR STORIES:

Devotional 34

Jesus chose you

TOPIC: Confidence

MAIN SCRIPTURES: "Very truly I tell you, whoever believes in me will do the works I have been doing, and they will do even greater things than these, because I am going to the Father." (John 14:12)

"When they saw the courage of Peter and John and realized that they were unschooled, ordinary men, they were astonished and they took note that these men had been with Jesus." (Acts 4:13)

OTHER SCRIPTURES: Matthew 16:18 – 19; Matthew 17:20; John 21:15 – 17; Acts 1:8; Ephesians 1:11 – 12, 19 – 20

WHAT JESUS MIGHT SAY TO YOU: Have you read my words to you in John 14:12? Do you understand what they mean? If so, you're probably feeling overwhelmed, right? "How on earth can I do greater things than Jesus, let alone the same things? I can't even get my own life together!"

I understand your feelings, and I want to encourage you.

Believe it or not, I chose you—to follow me, to be my friend and child, but also to be my coworker. I have faith in you. You're usually taught to have faith in me, but I'm telling you that I also have great faith in you. I would not have chosen you if I did not believe you could do what I do. I returned to heaven knowing that you're able to continue my work.

Look at the men I chose for disciples. They were unschooled ... and not successful, well – respected, or powerful men. But they became powerful because I worked through them. Although

Peter denied me three times, I chose him to feed my sheep and build my church.

Being my disciple means following me closely, learning from me, becoming like me, and doing what I do. This is what it means to abide. We become inseparable. As my child, you also have the Holy Spirit. You have God dwelling in you, giving you the ability to be like me and move mountains!

Don't underestimate yourself and who I've made you to be. When you are weak, I am strong. You are made in my image and filled with my Spirit … by whom you have access to the same power that raised me from the dead! You can be like me. I have faith in you. Trust me as I trust you.

Go be my disciple.

Follow my lead,

Jesus

HOW JESUS'S WORDS AFFECT MY STORY:

HOW I COULD AFFECT THEIR STORIES:

Devotional 35

embracing the mess

TOPIC: Brokenness

MAIN SCRIPTURES: "Each time he said, 'My grace is all you need. My power works best in weakness.' So now I am glad to boast about my weaknesses, so that the power of Christ can work through me." (2 Corinthians 12:9, NLT)

"This is real love—not that we loved God, but that he loved us and sent his Son as a sacrifice to take away our sins. Dear friends, since God loved us that much, we surely ought to love each other." (1 John 4:10–11, NLT)

OTHER SCRIPTURES: Matthew 9:11–13; Romans 7:15, 19–20; 2 Corinthians 1:4

WHAT JESUS MIGHT SAY TO YOU: Life on earth is messy, but I still love you. In the messy times. In the good times. As we understand and recognize that this is true, I want you to do the same thing for other people. When you run across someone who seems to be going through a difficult time, reach out to him or her. It could be something as simple as listening to the situation someone is in or recognizing a need—like clean water wells in Africa—and helping out. You have received my love; now I want you to offer it to those in need.

It's not just about helping people with their physical needs either. It's about loving them right where they are emotionally: a friend who made a poor decision, an outcast at school, a peer who has learning disabilities. Do you know why? Because they need me too, just like you did—just like you still do.

If you struggle with loving others who might be in a mess, ask me to let you feel what I feel when I look at your classmates or friends. That is a prayer I love to answer: to give you my heart for the hurting or broken.

All of mankind is pretty much in the same situation. Each person needs to know my love. When that happens, each of those loved people needs to pass along the good news. Then every day on earth will look a little more like every day in heaven.

Loving people with all that I am,

Jesus

HOW JESUS'S WORDS AFFECT MY STORY:

HOW I COULD AFFECT THEIR STORIES:

Devotional 36

don't fake out

TOPIC: Identity

MAIN SCRIPTURES: "Because we loved you so much, we were delighted to share with you not only the gospel of God but our lives as well." (1 Thessalonians 2:8)

"If we claim to be without sin, we deceive ourselves and the truth is not in us. If we confess our sins, he is faithful and just and will forgive us our sins and purify us from all unrighteousness." (1 John 1:8–9)

OTHER SCRIPTURES: Job 31:13–14; Daniel 3:16–18; Matthew 7:4–5; 1 Corinthians 9:22–23

WHAT JESUS MIGHT SAY TO YOU: When I was on earth, people expected a lot from me. They wanted me to be a savior based on what they thought a savior should be. But I didn't give in to the pressure. I knew exactly who I was and what I came to do — based on my Father's plans.

I want you to be real too. Don't put on a show. Don't pretend that you have it all together. Some people think that's what I want, a bunch of people all dressed in white, all acting according to a program. How boring would that be? I want you. I want the real thing.

Yes, that will be messy sometimes. You'll make a mistake or a bad choice, and you'll have to own that decision. You might need to tell a friend that you did the wrong thing or confess to your parents that you disobeyed. Do it. Be real. And not just with people; be real with me.

I know what's going on in your heart. I know your struggles and your sin and your messes. I love you still. So why not come to me, get it out of your heart, and move forward without that hanging over you? I paid a huge price on the cross for being myself and following what God asked me to do. But that reality and authenticity changed the world.

So be real with me and be real with others. Your friends need to know that this isn't a perfect journey—they need grace and they need to know they can find it in me. You'll be amazed how freeing it is not to have to hide who you are, from me or anyone else.

As real as it gets,

Jesus

HOW JESUS'S WORDS AFFECT MY STORY:

HOW I COULD AFFECT THEIR STORIES:

Devotional 37

love doesn't come easily

TOPIC: Loving Others

MAIN SCRIPTURE: "Follow God's example, therefore, as dearly loved children and walk in the way of love, just as Christ loved us and gave himself up for us as a fragrant offering and sacrifice to God." (Ephesians 5:1–2)

OTHER SCRIPTURES: Matthew 5:46–48; John 15:9, 12; 1 John 3:18

WHAT JESUS MIGHT SAY TO YOU: It's hard to love people sometimes, isn't it? Why is that? Could it be because your love may not be returned or because their response doesn't benefit you or make you feel valued?

Here's the bad news: Love is hard. The good news is, I can help.

Think of how often people reject my love. It breaks my heart every single time ... but I keep on loving them. Think of all the times you've disregarded me and chosen your own way. Even then I kept on loving you, no matter what.

Now I ask you to love others in this same way. My love will enable you to do this. My love is not dependent on outcome. True love is sacrificial. There's a cost. I gave my life because I love you. Love others because of me and as an offering to me, not because of what you anticipate in return. Love others the way I love you.

Don't let someone's response to your love determine your identity or self-worth. Let me determine your value. Be secure and content in my love. My love for you will never change. Let me be your anchor.

Love others for my sake and in my name. It will be hard, but it will be worth the struggle.

Let your love for others be unwavering, just like my love for you. Do not be shaken. Make me your first love. When this happens, my love will overflow to others through you. My love changes lives!

Let my love be your motivation and your strength.

Your source,

Jesus

HOW JESUS'S WORDS AFFECT MY STORY:

HOW I COULD AFFECT THEIR STORIES:

Devotional 38

safe heart, safe mind

TOPIC: Your Heart

MAIN SCRIPTURES: "Guard your heart above all else, for it determines the course of your life." (Proverbs 4:23, NLT)

"Create in me a pure heart, O God, and renew a steadfast spirit within me." (Psalm 51:10)

OTHER SCRIPTURES: Psalm 61:2; Mark 12:30; Ephesians 1:18–19

WHAT JESUS MIGHT SAY TO YOU: You are safest with me. Your heart is safest in my care. Unfortunately, on this planet, your heart is in danger from all kinds of enemies. The world wants to fill your heart with desire—desire for stuff, desire for people, desire for things you shouldn't have. Movies portray the idea that your heart is safest when given away to the guy or gal of your dreams. Chart-topping songs talk about broken hearts and quick fixes. And you have a real enemy who would like nothing more than for you to lose heart in me. He will try to tempt you in a thousand different ways to give your heart away to someone else or to many others in bits and pieces.

I will protect you from those things—if you let me. Keep me first in your life. Spend time with me, and let my love fill you up. I can't protect you if you fill your mind and heart with junk. Do whatever it takes to protect your love for me and my love for you. Guard your eyes as you watch TV or surf the Internet. Protect your ears from music that will draw your heart away, and be willing to wait before giving your heart to another person. Be careful about letting your emotions overpower decisions about friendships and dating.

Oh, don't get me wrong, I'm all about love and romance and finding someone to share your life with—but only under the safety of my protection. Be cautious. Let me love you. Love me in return. Then you'll be able to live and love without putting yourself in such terrible danger.

The great heart-protector,

Jesus

HOW JESUS'S WORDS AFFECT MY STORY:

HOW I COULD AFFECT THEIR STORIES:

Devotional 39

tuning in

TOPIC: Holy Spirit

MAIN SCRIPTURE: "The Spirit told Philip, 'Go to that chariot and stay near it.' Then Philip ran up to the chariot and heard the man reading Isaiah the prophet. 'Do you understand what you are reading?' Philip asked. 'How can I,' he said, 'unless someone explains it to me?' So he invited Philip to come up and sit with him." (Acts 8:29–31)

OTHER SCRIPTURES: 1 Kings 19:11–12; Matthew 10:19–20; Acts 1:8; Acts: 8:35–40; Acts 13:2–3; Acts 16:6–10; Acts 18:9–11; Acts 20:22

WHAT JESUS MIGHT SAY TO YOU: Do you know my voice? The Holy Spirit is my messenger; he always stays with you and he directs you in the way I want you to go. Don't worry if you struggle understanding me. It takes some time to learn how to listen. Just know that I talk to you on a spiritual level, in a deep place beyond surface emotions and thoughts. And everything I tell you will line up with what the Bible says. I will never tell you anything that goes against my word, although sometimes I may ask you to do things that feel risky. My disciple Philip didn't know who was in that chariot when I told him to go up to it and introduce himself. He had no idea that he'd be meeting a VIP from Ethiopia. The man served in the royal court, and I wanted Philip to be the one to tell him about me. Philip could have thought, *I don't know who that man is and I certainly can't keep up with a chariot.* But Philip listened to me because he was so in tune with how I speak that he knew my voice.

But Philip wasn't getting special privileges. I speak to all my followers. They just don't always listen. You'll know my voice if you spend time getting to know me. Read about other people I've spoken to, such as my disciples and my prophets. Study my words in the Bible. I'll never tell you to sin; I'll never tell you to do something that might hurt someone else. I'll tell you to do things that show compassion, truth, and love, and sometimes I may even tell you to be bold and tell someone about my love for them. When you know me well, then you'll recognize when I speak through my Spirit to your spirit. And as I talk and you listen, I'll use you to do great works.

Yes, I am speaking to you,

Jesus

HOW JESUS'S WORDS AFFECT MY STORY:

HOW I COULD AFFECT THEIR STORIES:

stumping the world

TOPIC: Serving Others

MAIN SCRIPTURE: "Then make me truly happy by agreeing wholeheartedly with each other, loving one another, and working together with one mind and purpose. Don't be selfish; don't try to impress others. Be humble, thinking of others as better than yourselves. Don't look out only for your own interests, but take an interest in others, too. You must have the same attitude that Christ Jesus had. Though he was God, he did not think of equality with God as something to cling to. Instead, he gave up his divine privileges; he took the humble position of a slave and was born as a human being. When he appeared in human form, he humbled himself in obedience to God and died a criminal's death on a cross." (Philippians 2:2 – 8, NLT)

OTHER SCRIPTURES: Mark 10:45; John 17:9 – 23; Galatians 6:9; 1 Peter 4:10

WHAT JESUS MIGHT SAY TO YOU: When I showed up on earth, people expected me to act a certain way, do all kinds of miracles, and display my supernatural power. They didn't expect me to be a servant. They didn't expect me to let rulers torture me and kill me. Most people didn't get me. They wanted me to dazzle them, to reveal my power like the next big superhero. As the most powerful man on earth, I could have done just that—but that wasn't why I came. I came to show a different way to live.

And that's the way I want you to live—differently. My way is the way of service. As my follower, I want you to get along so well with others that other people start wondering how you do it. As my follower, I want you to be so respectful that others are surprised when you don't demand your rights. Use your gifts for good rather than for success or recognition. Why is this my way? Because it's not the way of the world, which demands attention, elevates people, praises those who "get ahead," and honors the ambitious and self-serving. My way is to serve others. And following my way isn't hard. Care for others. Reach out when someone is in need. Especially look out for those who follow me; stick together even when you don't agree on everything. Show unity, because I am the one who brings you together. Don't let petty issues separate you from other God followers. I am watching, and I'll reward you.

Stump the world by following my example of serving others with humility. At some point, they'll start asking questions. When they do, you'll be able to point to me and tell them why you've chosen a different way.

Setting a different standard,

Jesus

HOW JESUS'S WORDS AFFECT MY STORY:

HOW I COULD AFFECT THEIR STORIES:

get it straight

TOPIC: Truth

MAIN SCRIPTURES: "Stand your ground, putting on the belt of truth and the body armor of God's righteousness." (Ephesians 6:14, NLT)

"But whoever lives by the truth comes into the light, so that it may be seen plainly that what they have done has been done in the sight of God." (John 3:21)

OTHER SCRIPTURES: Psalm 25:4–5; Isaiah 11:5; John 14:6; Ephesians 4:15, 25; 2 Peter 2:1–3; 1 John 1:5–10; 1 John 4:6; 3 John 1:3–4

WHAT JESUS MIGHT SAY TO YOU: You probably hear from parents or youth leaders that you need to spend time in my Word. I understand that it may feel like a chore, but reading the Bible is different than studying a textbook for school or reading some kind of owner's manual. It's more than checking a box on the list of "good things Christians should do." Reading the Bible is all about spending time with me and learning my ways so that you will be filled with truth. And here's reality: *I* am truth. Everything about me—the beauty of creation, my perfect ways, my love for you—all of it is right there in Scripture, written down for you.

Deception is the opposite of truth, and there's plenty of it out there. The enemy often takes pieces of truth and twists them ever so slightly so people fall for the lie. For instance, think about all the religions out there; most of them are based on the truth that God exists. But the twist is that god is someone or something other than me, Jesus Christ the Son of the one God. Deception even tricks people into ignoring the truth when it smacks them in the face.

So do you see how important knowing truth—knowing me— is for you? Truth equals light. Deception equals darkness. Any deception that pulls you in, whether it's a lie about my character or a lie that keeps you from my love, will bring darkness into your world. If you stick with me and get to know me, you'll be able to spot a lie a mile away. It won't even have a chance to deceive you. Truth will ground you and keep you secure; your mind and heart won't be swayed by anything.

Keeping it real,
Jesus

HOW JESUS'S WORDS AFFECT MY STORY:

HOW I COULD AFFECT THEIR STORIES:

making the grade

TOPIC: Righteousness

MAIN SCRIPTURE: "Therefore, put on every piece of God's armor so you will be able to resist the enemy in the time of evil. Then after the battle you will still be standing firm. Stand your ground, putting on the belt of truth and the body armor of God's righteousness." (Ephesians 6:13–14, NLT)

OTHER SCRIPTURES: Isaiah 11:5; Isaiah 59:17; Isaiah 61:10–11; Romans 3:21–26; 1 Corinthians 1:30–31; 2 Corinthians 5:17–21

WHAT JESUS MIGHT SAY TO YOU: Did you know that when you chose to believe in me, it changed your standing with God? You went from a sinful state to good standing. It was like you had a failing grade beforehand, then you automatically had a 4.0 GPA without doing a thing to earn it. God no longer saw your sin or your failures. He saw you as righteous—you are right with him because of me.

This righteousness is now a protective armor for you. My life acts like a shield, guarding you from those who would try to destroy you with temptation and sin. Watch out; it's easy to forget that this armor of righteousness is here for you. Every day you'll hear lies about who you are and who I am. Those lies may tempt you to drop your guard or forget your shield, but don't let that happen. Remember that I saved your life from eternal failure, and hold on to that reality. I made amends with God on your behalf.

So every day put on my armor of righteousness like you would put on a coat to protect you from a blizzard or like shin guards and knee pads for hockey. My righteousness will help you boldly face the lies with truth. Your mind will be rock solid. Your heart will be grounded. You will be ready for any temptation or attack that comes your way.

My righteousness becomes your righteousness. Your sins don't count against you anymore. You've gone from condemned to accepted. That means I can shield you with my strength. To mess with you, your enemies have to go through me. And as long as you keep me close, that's not going to happen.

Your righteousness,

Jesus

HOW JESUS'S WORDS AFFECT MY STORY:

HOW I COULD AFFECT THEIR STORIES:

pass the peace, please

TOPIC: Peace

MAIN SCRIPTURES: "For shoes, put on the peace that comes from the Good News so that you will be fully prepared." (Ephesians 6:15 NLT)

"How beautiful on the mountains are the feet of the messenger who brings good news, the good news of peace and salvation, the news that the God of Israel reigns!" (Isaiah 52:7, NLT)

OTHER SCRIPTURES: Ephesians 2:14; 2 Timothy 2:22; 1 Peter 3:8 – 12

WHAT JESUS MIGHT SAY TO YOU: I am the ultimate peacemaker. Before antiwar movements started and people thought it was cool to march and hold up signs for peace, I was all about it. Remember my death on the cross? I did that to bring peace between God and sinful people. You and he were on opposite sides, so I made a big sacrifice to change the relationship.

Now that you are at peace with God, how can you bring peace to others in my name? When people insult you, don't insult them back. When others want to fight, walk away. When others disagree with you, respect them without riling them up. When someone hurts you, bless him or her. Give kind words.

Peacemakers enjoy life and relationships. They know how to soothe an angry person and respond with gentleness. Peacemaking takes brains because you really have to think before you speak, pause before you act, and wait before you respond. Peacemakers understand self-control. If you aim for peace, you'll realize that instead of standing up for yourself, the better way may be to say nothing at all. It sounds difficult, and sometimes it is, but peace is part of my good news. I turned you from being an enemy of God into his friend; now you can help others find the same peace with him.

When my peace rules your mind, then bringing peace to other situations will come naturally. You'll start looking for ways to be a peacemaker even before situations turn into all-out wars. Start today by thinking about a relationship that's been difficult for you. Turn the situation around by being honest. If you can't find it in your heart to want peace with that person, then talk to me. I'm in the business of changing hearts, and as we spend time together I can change yours too.

The originator of peace,

Jesus

HOW JESUS'S WORDS AFFECT MY STORY:

HOW I COULD AFFECT THEIR STORIES:

Devotional 44

protection from temptation

TOPIC: Faith

MAIN SCRIPTURE: "Therefore, put on every piece of God's armor so you will be able to resist the enemy in the time of evil. Then after the battle you will still be standing firm ... Hold up the shield of faith to stop the fiery arrows of the devil." (Ephesians 6:13, 16, NLT)

OTHER SCRIPTURES: Psalm 18; Psalm 28:7; Proverbs 18:10; Isaiah 42:3; Romans 8:31–39; 1 Corinthians 10:13; Ephesians 2:8–9; 1 Thessalonians 5:8; Hebrews 11; 1 Peter 5:8–9; 1 John 5:4–5

WHAT JESUS MIGHT SAY TO YOU: Do you remember when you were younger and cried out for protection from someone intent on hurting you? What you needed was a protector, a shield from the enemy's attack.

Now that you're older, the dangers you face go much deeper than the threat of physical pain. Every day you encounter temptations that are like poisonous arrows aimed at your soul—arrows that deaden your conscience, rob your innocence, and harden your heart toward me; arrows of doubt, despair, compromise, and selfishness.

I know you feel overwhelmed by the pressure to conform to the standards of this world. But how do you withstand these attacks on your soul?

Lift up your shield of faith. I'm your shield. Your shelter. Your strong tower. Your protector. Place your faith in my power to help you. Call out to me, and I will make a way through any firestorm of temptation. Without me you can't overcome, but with me you are more than a conqueror.

Nothing can touch you except what comes through me — because I'm in control. You may seem overwhelmed by the temptations you're facing, but trust me — I won't let anything happen to you that you can't handle.

So cry out to me and look to me for help because I long to rescue you. And know that when you lift up your shield of faith, you lift up me.

Your shield,

Jesus

HOW JESUS'S WORDS AFFECT MY STORY:

HOW I COULD AFFECT THEIR STORIES:

it's all about him

TOPIC: Salvation

MAIN SCRIPTURE: "Therefore, put on every piece of God's armor so you will be able to resist the enemy in the time of evil. Then after the battle you will still be standing firm ... Put on salvation as your helmet, and take the sword of the Spirit, which is the word of God." (Ephesians 6:13, 17, NLT)

OTHER SCRIPTURES: Deuteronomy 31:8; Psalm 27:1; Isaiah 59:17; Isaiah 61:10; Ephesians 1:3–14; Colossians 1:15–20; Colossians 3:1–4; 1 Thessalonians 5:8

WHAT JESUS MIGHT SAY TO YOU: It's all about me. No, really. You wouldn't exist if I hadn't created you. You wouldn't know me if I hadn't made myself known to you first. And you wouldn't be able to receive the gift of eternal life if I hadn't died on the cross for your sins. I am your salvation.

It works to your advantage that it's all about me. If life were all about you, then your salvation would depend on you. You would spend the rest of your life earning the right to spend eternity with me. You would live in fear of never measuring up and maybe not going to heaven after you die. But all you need to do—all you can do—is put on the helmet of salvation. *My* salvation.

Satan will do whatever he can to convince you that your salvation is all about you. But by putting on the helmet of salvation, you protect yourself from his assaults.

When you mess up, trust in the power of my blood to cleanse you from the stain of sin. When you doubt if you'll ever be good enough, trust in my good work on the cross to save you. When you're afraid that you've strayed too far to find your way back home, trust in my promise that I will never leave you nor forsake you.

So stop trying to be good enough. Stop beating yourself up. Stop worrying about the possibility of losing your salvation. Put on the helmet of salvation and trust that you will spend eternity with me not because of the good or bad things you've done, but because of what I've done for you. And know this: by putting on the helmet of salvation, you are putting on me.

Your salvation,

Jesus

HOW JESUS'S WORDS AFFECT MY STORY:

HOW I COULD AFFECT THEIR STORIES:

your only weapon

TOPIC: Sword of the Spirit

MAIN SCRIPTURE: "Therefore, put on every piece of God's armor so you will be able to resist the enemy in the time of evil. Then after the battle you will still be standing firm ... Put on salvation as your helmet, and take the sword of the Spirit, which is the word of God." (Ephesians 6:13, 17, NLT)

OTHER SCRIPTURES: Psalm 119:11; Isaiah 40:8; Luke 4:1 – 12; John 1:14; Hebrews 4:12 – 13; Revelation 1:16; Revelation 12:11; Revelation 19:15

WHAT JESUS MIGHT SAY TO YOU: Every day our relationship faces continuous attacks from Satan. Through greed, selfishness, dishonesty, sexual compromise, and a host of other sins, Satan is intent on destroying what you and I have.

In your battle against Satan and the forces of evil, I have given you one weapon to strike back with: the sword of the Spirit, which is the Word of God.

At my weakest point during my time on earth, Satan tempted me to sacrifice everything for a shortcut to power, fame, and provision. And believe me, the temptation was great. But in that moment I pulled out my sword of the Spirit and struck back. Rather than rely on profound arguments or scientific proofs, I quoted the Word of God.

When you face temptation in your greatest moment of weakness, when your friends or your teachers attack our relationship, when you face discouragement and despair that make you wonder if life is worth living … strike back with the sword of the Spirit. Be careful not to use it to hurt or demean others, but rely on it as your primary resource in responding to whatever attacks you encounter—whether they come directly from Satan or through people around you.

When you spend time in my Word, you also spend time with me because I am God's Word in human form.

So lift up the sword of the Spirit and know that when you do, you also lift me up.

Your sword,

Jesus

HOW JESUS'S WORDS AFFECT MY STORY:

HOW I COULD AFFECT THEIR STORIES:

Devotional 47

lean on me

TOPIC: Trusting God

MAIN SCRIPTURE: "Trust in the LORD with all your heart and lean not on your own understanding; in all your ways submit to him, and he will make your paths straight." (Proverbs 3:5–6)

OTHER SCRIPTURES: 2 Kings 18:5; Psalm 31:13–15; Daniel 3:28; Colossians 2:7–10

WHAT JESUS MIGHT SAY TO YOU: How much do you really trust me? I know it would be easier if I showed up in person and sat with you as you prayed, or if in the moment you called out I appeared in a bright light to rescue you. But you need to know something: I am here. I do hear your cries. I'm always with you. And I want to open your spiritual eyes so that you can know and feel my presence—but you have to trust me.

Trust is relying on me, and it's part of faith. So while you may trust me for your salvation, I want to take it further than that. Let's talk about trusting me with your day-to-day life. When you're at school. When you're making or losing friends. When people are cruel to you, or when your family is falling apart. Will you trust me?

Part of trust is knowing that I'm always at work, even when you can't see it. Sometimes you won't understand what's happening around you. I may even allow things that totally confuse you—like letting your parents split up, or not intervening when friends stop being friends. Those kinds of things may not seem like I'm taking care of you. But I am. I am still with you during those times. I will comfort you and give you wisdom to handle rough situations. Trust that I really am God and I'm really in charge, even when it doesn't make sense. If you can trust me like that, then you'll find my peace and comfort. You'll start seeing life from the big picture, beyond what you see right here, right now.

Ready to try it? I'll show up. I always do.

Waiting for your trust,

Jesus

HOW JESUS'S WORDS AFFECT MY STORY:

HOW I COULD AFFECT THEIR STORIES:

Devotional 48

talking to God 24/7

TOPIC: Prayer

MAIN SCRIPTURE: "Do not be anxious about anything, but in every situation, by prayer and petition, with thanksgiving, present your requests to God." (Philippians 4:6)

OTHER SCRIPTURES: Luke 18:1 – 7; Romans 8:26 – 27; Galatians 4:6; Philippians 4:6 – 7; 1 Thessalonians 5:17; Jude v. 20

WHAT JESUS MIGHT SAY TO YOU: Despite the intensity of a spiritual battle or how strong or weak you feel at any given moment, I have given you everything you need to live a godly life and to stand your ground against any attack from your Enemy, Satan.

With every piece of spiritual armor you put on, you clothe yourself with me. I am your helmet of salvation, your breastplate of righteousness, your belt of truth, your shoes of the good news of peace, your sword of the Spirit.

But wearing your spiritual armor still isn't enough. If you run into battle fully equipped but aren't in communication with your command center, you will lose. You need my guidance, my wisdom, my encouragement, and my strength. That's why it's important that you pray at all times and on every occasion in the power of the Holy Spirit.

Praying at all times means staying in constant communication with me: When you wake up, in between classes, during a test at school, while you're hanging out with your friends, when you go to bed. Prayer is more of an attitude than an activity. Satan loves to ambush my unsuspecting followers. Without prayer he will catch you off guard every time.

As you pray, avoid doing all the talking. I know you have a lot on your heart, but make room for the Holy Spirit to guide you in prayer. Spend time in silence so I can respond to you. But also remember that you're in the middle of a war, not just a fight. Other people face the same attacks as you. They need you to pray for them as much as you need them to pray for you.

But there's one more reason why we need to stay connected: I just like to spend time with you!

Your source for everything,

Jesus

HOW JESUS'S WORDS AFFECT MY STORY:

HOW I COULD AFFECT THEIR STORIES:

Devotional 49

make peace with your past

TOPIC: Regret

MAIN SCRIPTURE: "God saved you by his grace when you believed. And you can't take credit for this; it is a gift from God. Salvation is not a reward for the good things we have done, so none of us can boast about it. For we are God's masterpiece. He has created us anew in Christ Jesus, so we can do the good things he planned for us long ago." (Ephesians 2:8–10, NLT)

OTHER SCRIPTURES: Psalm 103:10–14; Ezekiel 36:26–27; Acts 22:1–21; Romans 5:8; 2 Corinthians 1:3–4; 2 Corinthians 5:17; 1 John 1:7

WHAT JESUS MIGHT SAY TO YOU: No matter how hard you try to hide it, ignore it, even fix it, you can't change your past. And I don't want you to, because your past—your failures as well as your successes—makes you who you are.

Even when you thought you were all alone, I was with you: in your darkest hour, when you committed your most embarrassing sin, in the middle of your greatest humiliation.

I know the real you, and I died to free you from the chains of your past. You are now a new creation; the old has passed away and the new has come. Your past sins are completely wiped away from my memory.

But I will not erase your past from your memory because your scars can serve as reminders of my presence in your darkest hours. The memory of your most embarrassing sin tells you how much you need my forgiveness. The moments of your greatest humiliation remind you of the humiliation I endured to free you from your past and your sins of the present. And besides, how can you see how far I've brought you unless you have something to compare it to? Rather than grow bitter or embarrassed by your history, use it as an opportunity to grow closer to me. Use your experiences—both good and bad—to comfort others who are walking the same road you have walked.

Your Redeemer,

Jesus

HOW JESUS'S WORDS AFFECT MY STORY:

HOW I COULD AFFECT THEIR STORIES:

be the friend you'd want to have

TOPIC: Friendship

MAIN SCRIPTURE: "How beloved and gracious were Saul and Jonathan! They were together in life and in death. They were swifter than eagles, stronger than lions." (2 Samuel 1:23, NLT)

OTHER SCRIPTURES: 1 Samuel 16:7; 1 Samuel 20:42; Proverbs 13:20; Proverbs 17:17; Ecclesiastes 4:9–12; John 15:12–15; Philippians 2:1–11

WHAT JESUS MIGHT SAY TO YOU: I understand your desire for a friend. Here are a few thoughts to help you find one.

If you wait for a good friend to materialize suddenly before your eyes, you may have to wait forever. The best way to find a friend is to be one.

Look around you: Who do you already know that might need a friend? Don't judge people by their outward appearance—my Father in heaven sure doesn't. He looks at the heart. In the same way, you may be surprised that people you assume would drive you nuts might actually grow on you once you get to know them.

The people who became my friends during my time on earth didn't fit the job description of the "proper" friends for the Son of God. They included tax collectors and fishermen—not exactly the most respected people back in my days on earth.

Let's look a little deeper into what kind of a friend you might want to be. Take a few moments and ask yourself, "What kind of a friend has Jesus been to me?" Hopefully words such as *loving*, *accepting*, and *forgiving* come to mind. Those qualities will serve you well in being—and finding—a friend. A good friend has the heart of a servant and is willing to sacrifice. Who wouldn't want a friend like that?

Don't get discouraged because you haven't found the right friend. Acquaintances are easy to find, but lasting friendships take time. In the meantime be the kind of friend to those around you that I am to you.

Your best friend,

Jesus

HOW JESUS'S WORDS AFFECT MY STORY:

HOW I COULD AFFECT THEIR STORIES:

Devotional 51

too soon to quit

TOPIC: Encouragement

MAIN SCRIPTURE: "God also bound himself with an oath, so that those who received the promise could be perfectly sure that he would never change his mind. So God has given both his promise and his oath. These two things are unchangeable because it is impossible for God to lie. Therefore, we who have fled to him for refuge can have great confidence as we hold to the hope that lies before us." (Hebrews 6:17 – 18, NLT)

OTHER SCRIPTURES: Psalm 138:3, 7 – 8; Isaiah 43:2; Isaiah 51:12

WHAT JESUS MIGHT SAY TO YOU: Living for me is like running a long race. Are you full of energy today or so tired you can hardly keep your legs moving? Life is more uphill than downhill. More headwind than tailwind. I lived here. I know how exhausting it can be.

But you're not running this race alone. Look for me standing beside the track. Do you see me? I'm cheering for you. It's too soon to quit. I'll give you extra strength to keep going and finish the race. I know you can do it with my help.

When you pray about your struggles every day, I hear your prayers and answer them. Read my Word and drink in my encouragement and strength. When you're surrounded by trouble or struggling with problems, I won't abandon you. I will be with you and bring you through. I made you. I won't let you be destroyed.

Don't be overwhelmed by any problem another person drops on you. You can handle it with my help. I calm your spirit and give you the confidence to face anything. Receive my encouragement and hold fast to hope until you see me face-to-face.

And don't keep all my encouragement to yourself! Spread some around. Build others up. Give love and care to the weak. Affirm those who doubt themselves. Be thankful in every situation. Cheer for your friends as I cheer for you. The more you give away, the more I will give to you. Your friends will ask where you get such a positive attitude and the grit to keep going. Tell them they can have it, too, if they come to me.

Cheering you on,

Jesus

HOW JESUS'S WORDS AFFECT MY STORY:

HOW I COULD AFFECT THEIR STORIES:

Devotional 52

cleaned up

TOPIC: Past Mistakes

MAIN SCRIPTURE: "I have not achieved it, but I focus on this one thing: Forgetting the past and looking forward to what lies ahead." (Philippians 3:13, NLT)

OTHER SCRIPTURES: Psalm 103:11 – 12; Romans 3:25; Romans 12:1 – 2; 2 Corinthians 5:17

WHAT JESUS MIGHT SAY TO YOU: When you gave your life to me, I forgave everything in your past. Completely. Absolutely everything. All the dirt from your past, present, and future is washed away. Though your sins seem as scarlet they shall be as white as snow. My blood is a stain remover that wipes your life clean. Everything is forgiven.

In your shame, your past defined who you were. Satan lied to you and personalized your sin. He accused you and called you a thief, a drunk, a hypocrite, whatever. If you believe that, you give him permission to keep you chained to your past.

In me you are a new creation. The old is gone. The new has come.

Your new life is defined by my righteousness. You are made good by me—by my blood. When I died, your sin was taken from you and poured into me. My righteousness (right standing with God) was poured into you. God has removed your sins as far away from you as the east is far from the west.

Your new life is not about your past. Your new focus is on the future and your new life with me. You willingly presented yourself to me as a living sacrifice, so I can do with you whatever I want. And here's what I want—stop copying the behaviors and patterns of this world. Be a new and different person with a new freshness in all you do and think. Be like me. You will find out how satisfying this really is. It's what you were created to be.

Your righteousness,

Jesus

HOW JESUS'S WORDS AFFECT MY STORY:

HOW I COULD AFFECT THEIR STORIES:

Devotional 53

songs that rock the charts

TOPIC: God's Love

MAIN SCRIPTURE: "The LORD your God is with you, the Mighty Warrior who saves. He will take great delight in you; in his love he will no longer rebuke you, but will rejoice over you with singing." (Zephaniah 3:17)

OTHER SCRIPTURES: Psalm 18:19; John 15:13–16; Romans 8:31–35

WHAT JESUS MIGHT SAY TO YOU: This might come as a surprise, but I sing over you, and truth be told, I have a pretty good voice. I think you would like your song. Sometimes I sing it over you as you sleep, quieting your heart. Other times my song is loud and joyful, with a strong beat that makes my heart dance. I can't help but sing; my love just overflows and comes out in song.

One day I'll let you hear it.

I pray for you too. Whenever you are going through a rough spot, whenever you're facing temptation or when life feels overwhelming, I call out to my Father on your behalf. I like to speak of your name to my Father, because we both love you more than you know. Nothing can ever separate you from our love; nothing you ever go through can keep our love away.

I want you to know that my kind of love, expressed through song and prayer, and through my very life, has the ability to strengthen you. My love has power: power to win over temptation, power to hold you up in a hardship, power to bring hope when it feels like you're lost. And just think, if I was willing to give my life for you, don't you think I can help with anything and everything else you face?

All that I do should be a constant reminder of how much I think of you, how eager I am to rescue you. You mean the world to me.

Singing about you,

Jesus

HOW JESUS'S WORDS AFFECT MY STORY:

HOW I COULD AFFECT THEIR STORIES:

the rumor of Jesus

TOPIC: Making Jesus Contagious

MAIN SCRIPTURE: "A man was there by the name of Zacchaeus; he was a chief tax collector and was wealthy. He wanted to see who Jesus was, but because he was short he could not see over the crowd. So he ran ahead and climbed a sycamore-fig tree to see him, since Jesus was coming that way. When Jesus reached the spot, he looked up and said to him, 'Zacchaeus, come down immediately. I must stay at your house today.' So he came down at once and welcomed him gladly. All the people saw this and began to mutter, 'He has gone to be the guest of a sinner.' But Zacchaeus stood up and said to the Lord, 'Look, Lord! Here and now I give half of my possessions to the poor, and if I have cheated anybody out of anything, I will pay back four times the amount.' Jesus said to him, 'Today salvation has come to this house, because this man, too, is a son of Abraham. For the Son of Man came to seek and to save the lost.'" (Luke 19:2 – 10)

OTHER SCRIPTURES: Matthew 5:15 – 16; John 13:35

WHAT JESUS MIGHT SAY TO YOU: Who was Zacchaeus, and why was he so eager to see me? What had he heard about me? Who did he hear from? Why was he so intrigued by me?

He was a tax collector and considered a big-time sinner in his day, yet he was straining to see me. Why? He had never met me, but he had obviously heard of me. And whatever he heard was some-thing so moving, so compelling, that he just had to see me for himself.

Zacchaeus must have heard about me from someone ... or seen the evidence of me in someone's life. And it made him wonder. So I have a few questions for you: *Is the rumor of me so powerfully evident in your life that people long to meet me after spending time with you? Does your life make people want to climb trees and scale mountains just to get a glimpse of my face?*

When I was on earth, undesirables flocked to me. I was even called a "friend of sinners." These days sinners shy away from those who claim to follow me. Why is that? Are you doing something to counteract this?

Do you cause people to run to me, or are you like the disciples, grumbling and saying, "He has gone in to be the guest of a man who is a sinner" (Luke 19:7, ESV)? Does my love flow through you to others?

When you run to me as Zacchaeus did and understand your need for me, you'll be changed by my love, and my love will become evident in your life. When people spend time with you and experience this love, they will be attracted to my love as Zacchaeus was.

Live a life of contagious love!

Pursuing you always,

Jesus

HOW JESUS'S WORDS AFFECT MY STORY:

HOW I COULD AFFECT THEIR STORIES:

Devotional 55

whining for more

TOPIC: Jealousy

MAIN SCRIPTURE: "But if you are bitterly jealous and there is selfish ambition in your heart, don't cover up the truth with boasting and lying. For jealousy and selfishness are not God's kind of wisdom. Such things are earthly, unspiritual, and demonic. For wherever there is jealousy and selfish ambition, there you will find disorder and evil of every kind." (James 3:14–16, NLT)

OTHER SCRIPTURES: Genesis 4:3–7; Proverbs 14:30; 1 Corinthians 13:4; 1 Timothy 6:3–5; James 1:17

WHAT JESUS MIGHT SAY TO YOU: Jealousy is sneaky. It even happened back when I was walking the earth. I'd been teaching my disciples every day, but still they used to stumble over this one. One time I caught them fighting over who was going to sit next to me in heaven. They were jealous of each other and wanted the best spot for themselves. I had to set them straight and remind them that it's not like that with me. I care about serving people, about loving them where they are — not ruling over them as an arrogant king with my mighty disciples. I want my followers today to have the same kind of attitude.

Caring about popularity and prestige is a quick way to land in a heap of trouble. The world will define popularity one way, and if that's what you are hungry for, you will end up making decisions you regret. The easiest way to avoid jealousy and its pitfalls is to be thankful for what you have. Don't worry if someone is better in sports or someone else has a lot of money. Don't spend a lot of time wishing for greater popularity or lots of stuff. None of that will get you anywhere anyway. If you're wrestling with this one, come to me. Talk to me. Tell me your longings and worries and let me help you see the bigger picture and find thankfulness for what I've given you.

Set aside anything that stirs up jealousy, envy, or pride, and let me work in your heart to remind you of the things that really matter.

Better than the "next big thing,"

Jesus

HOW JESUS'S WORDS AFFECT MY STORY:

HOW I COULD AFFECT THEIR STORIES:

Devotional 56

the jealousy trap

TOPIC: Envy

MAIN SCRIPTURE: "But if you are bitterly jealous and there is selfish ambition in your heart, don't cover up the truth with boasting and lying. For jealousy and selfishness are not God's kind of wisdom. Such things are earthly, unspiritual, and demonic. For wherever there is jealousy and selfish ambition, there you will find disorder and evil of every kind." (James 3:14–16, NLT)

OTHER SCRIPTURES: Genesis 4:3–7; Proverbs 14:30; 1 Corinthians 13:4; Galatians 5:19–21; 1 Timothy 6:3–7; James 4:1–3

WHAT JESUS MIGHT SAY TO YOU: People sure do complain a lot. You probably have your moments too. Ever had a friend who is always griping? It gets old, doesn't it? Gripes come from discontent. Discontent usually comes from jealousy, seeing what someone else has and wanting it for your own. Or jealousy may be wishing you were someone else or somewhere else. This kind of thinking can lead to trouble, so watch out for it.

Jealousy or envy digs into your heart and starts to grow bitterness. Once bitterness sprouts, it will turn your tongue into a sharp tool that inflicts damage. Jealousy and bitterness then feed on pride—you'll feel like you deserve the good things that you see other people getting. You'll wonder why they've got it so good and you don't. I hope you can see how dangerous this jealousy thing can be. It doesn't just remain a jealousy issue; it can turn into fights, severed ties, unhappiness, and on and on.

The key is to remember that I have a plan for everyone's life, whether he or she accepts it. So that means that what you have is what I've given. Where you are is where I've put you. Who you are is who I made you to be. Sure, sin messes things up and causes problems, but that doesn't mean I'm no longer in control.

So when you see me giving good things to others, be happy for them, praise me for blessing others, and remember that I give all good things—even if those things are going to other people.

Giving you what you need,

Jesus

HOW JESUS'S WORDS AFFECT MY STORY:

HOW I COULD AFFECT THEIR STORIES:

Devotional 57

rescue from darkness

TOPIC: Depression

MAIN SCRIPTURE: "O Lord, you alone are my hope. I've trusted you, O LORD, from childhood." (Psalm 71:5, NLT)

OTHER SCRIPTURES: Job 19:25–27; Psalm 23; Isaiah 60:1–2; Isaiah 61:1–3; Lamentations 3:21–24; Matthew 18:20; John 11:25; John 16:33; 1 Peter 1:3

WHAT JESUS MIGHT SAY TO YOU: You feel as if you're swimming all alone in an ocean of darkness and despair. After treading water for so long, you're ready to give up and let depression's undertow drag you to unknown places, perhaps even death.

My friend, this is not the life I designed for you. You cannot free yourself from pain and hardship, but my desire is not that you spend your life drowning in an ocean of depression.

Please don't swim alone. You need to share how you feel with an adult you trust who can keep you afloat in the water, such as a parent, a teacher, or a youth pastor or volunteer.

It's also important to surround yourself with people who care about you. I know your depression tells you that no one cares, but I have placed people in your life who want to encourage you. To avoid assuming that they know what's going on inside, make sure you explain in detail how you feel.

Anytime two or three people gather in my name, I am present in a way that I am present nowhere else. That's why spending time with other people who follow me will help provide a net to pull you out of the water.

The night before I was nailed to the cross, I cried out to my Father and asked him if there was any way I could be delivered from the pain I was about to suffer. The stress was so great that I began sweating drops of blood.

The good news is this: I know your depression, and I carried it with me on the cross. You no longer have to carry it, so give it to me. I endured the cross so I could be your resurrection and life.

Believe my good news,

Jesus

HOW JESUS'S WORDS AFFECT MY STORY:

HOW I COULD AFFECT THEIR STORIES:

failure puts you in good company

TOPIC: Failure

MAIN SCRIPTURE: "But he said to me, 'My grace is sufficient for you, for my power is made perfect in weakness.' Therefore I will boast all the more gladly about my weaknesses, so that Christ's power may rest on me. That is why, for Christ's sake, I delight in weaknesses, in insults, in hardships, in persecutions, in difficulties. For when I am weak, then I am strong." (2 Corinthians 12:9–10)

OTHER SCRIPTURES: Mark 14:66–72; John 21:15–19; Romans 3:23; Romans 8:1–11; Hebrews 12:1–2

WHAT JESUS MIGHT SAY TO YOU: So you messed up again. Would it help to know that you're in good company? In my greatest hour of need all of my disciples either betrayed me or abandoned me. In fact, every person who sought to follow my Father in heaven has messed up badly: Moses, Abraham, Sarah, David, Mary Magdalene, Paul, and many more.

I say this not so you'll take sin lightly; sin is serious, and your sin cost me my life. But how can I reject you? You're family! You belong to me because I purchased you with my blood on the cross. So stop beating yourself up and questioning whether I've rejected you.

But here's what I want you to do: Admit that you can't live up to my standards. I would rather you know how messed up you are than for you to be messed up and not realize it.

Look to me for strength. My power is made perfect in weakness. As long as you try to will yourself into obeying me, you won't be able to do it.

Let me live through you. You can't live a godly life, but I can, and I've made my home in the deepest place of your heart. Abide with me, yield yourself to me, and make me the focus of your life. And don't focus on your sin.

Brush yourself off and get back in the race. Don't give up just because you stumbled. Life is not a sprint, it's a marathon—so get up and keep on running!

Your failures will only make you stronger if you choose to respond to them correctly. But don't ever forget: You will never wear out my willingness to forgive you.

Your strength,

Jesus

HOW JESUS'S WORDS AFFECT MY STORY:

HOW I COULD AFFECT THEIR STORIES:

Devotional 59

safe sex

TOPIC: Sexual Boundaries

MAIN SCRIPTURE: "Daughters of Jerusalem, I charge you: Do not arouse or awaken love until it so desires." (Song of Solomon 8:4)

OTHER SCRIPTURES: Psalm 119:9; John 10:10; 1 Corinthians 6:18–20; Ephesians 5:1–20; Hebrews 13:4

WHAT JESUS MIGHT SAY TO YOU: I see the sexual messages society repeatedly tries to pound into your head. Society wants you to think that sex is simply a physical act, that there's nothing wrong with premarital sex. Don't believe it.

I'll get straight to the point: Premarital sex is sin. I'm not trying to make life miserable for you, but your heart isn't ready to handle the intimacy of a sexual relationship. Awakening your heart before the time is right will have devastating effects—including in your life with the person you eventually marry. Trust me.

So let's construct some boundaries together before you pass the point of no return:

1. Invite me into your relationships. I didn't come so you would have an unsatisfying life; I came so you might have an abundant life. And besides, I'm present in all your relationships—don't you think it's about time you acknowledge me in them? Make me an active part in your conversation, and you'll discover a spiritual dimension of your relationship that few couples enjoy.

2. Don't ask how far you can go. When you do that, you're looking for ways to get around me. Instead, stay far enough from the boundary that you won't have to ask that question. (Of course, asking me for a little insight doesn't hurt.)

3. Take time to get to know the other person. Usually when a premarital relationship becomes sexual, the two people stop exploring each other's hearts.

4. Do things in groups. This will go a long way toward preventing you from placing yourself in compromising positions.

5. Ask your friends to help you stay pure. They're an important line of defense.

You have a lifetime of enjoyable sex ahead of you. Don't put it in jeopardy by prematurely exploring it. And remember: If you've already explored, I love you just the same as I always have — just ask for my forgiveness and start your life and relationships anew.

Love,

Jesus

HOW JESUS'S WORDS AFFECT MY STORY:

HOW I COULD AFFECT THEIR STORIES:

Devotional 60

what's the proof?

TOPIC: Heaven and Hell

MAIN SCRIPTURE: "My Father's house has many rooms; if that were not so, would I have told you that I am going there to prepare a place for you? And if I go and prepare a place for you, I will come back and take you to be with me that you also may be where I am." (John 14:2–3)

OTHER SCRIPTURES: Matthew 7:13–14; Mark 9:43–48; 2 Corinthians 5:6–10; 1 Thessalonians 1:5–10; Hebrews 11:13–16; James 1:17

WHAT JESUS MIGHT SAY TO YOU: It's so easy to assume that this life is all there is. Believing in something or someone you cannot see or touch or smell requires faith. But heaven and hell are real places, and their existence affects your daily life.

Every time someone cuts you down, every time you stretch the truth or tell a lie, every time you prefer yourself to others, every time you do what you know is wrong, you prove the existence of hell. You see, hell isn't just a faraway place that "bad" people go to. Hell and Satan are the source of all evil in the world. And deep inside, your sinful nature craves this place—but it will only destroy your heart and drive you away from me.

Every time you encourage someone, every time you tell the truth (even when it hurts), every time you prefer others to yourself, every time you do what you know is right, you prove the existence of heaven. Heaven isn't a faraway place, either. Everything good and right and beautiful comes from my Father in heaven. Deep inside, your redeemed spirit craves this place, and as you draw closer to me, you will recognize other glimpses of heaven in your life.

The existence of good and evil in this world proves that heaven and hell exist because they must come from somewhere—or someone.

Your way, your truth, and your life,

Jesus

HOW JESUS'S WORDS AFFECT MY STORY:

HOW I COULD AFFECT THEIR STORIES:

Keep the Conversation Going

Now that you've spent time listening to Jesus and talking with him, don't stop. Chat, vent, pray, yell, whisper, praise—hold a conversation with him every day. These conversations will strengthen your faith, prepare you for challenges, and show you how to help others. While Jesus was on earth, he talked with everyone—those who followed him and those who did not, those who were sick, the demon-possessed and demons themselves, those who were hurting, religious leaders, rulers and royalty, the poor and the needy. He talks with anyone who will listen, and he offers life and freedom to everyone.

Ask him about anything. Put God's words to the test. He is the most reliable, faithful friend—and he rules the world. You couldn't ask for a better companion and guide. Plus, he gives his Holy Spirit to guide you.

Continue digging into God's story; his story affects yours, and his ways and power shape you and those around you. Everyone's story intertwines with God's. Your story could be the way friends and family are introduced to Jesus. Remember that the 3Story concept is first and always about abiding in Christ, taking your life breath from him, living your life through him, and loving and listening to him first, always with the help of his Holy Spirit.

Here's to many more talks that matter.

How 3Story Will Help You Share Your Faith

As you talk more with Jesus and pay attention to the stories around you, a few things about the 3Story concept will help you tell others about your faith in Jesus:

- 3Story is about bringing three stories together in a natural way. It is not about taking people through a sequence of predetermined steps.

- Focus on being honest, not on being perfect.

- Allow your friends to be who they are as you discover their stories.

- Ask questions rather than trying to give answers.

- Practice listening, not preaching. 3Story is built on the assumption that people listen to people who listen.

- Share about your need for Jesus and your hope in him rather than judging others' lifestyles, words, or choices.

- Let God's Spirit guide you in your relationships, instead of working through tips or techniques to maneuver God into a conversation.

- 3Story is about bringing Jesus's story into a relationship at just the right moment.

- Invite people to discover parts of Jesus's story that are most relevant to them at that moment. Jesus's story doesn't come to everybody in the same order or with the same words.

- Let love change people's hearts. Not only in a postmodern world but also from a biblical worldview, love rather than knowledge wins people's hearts.

- Don't worry about controlling conversations; rather, allow conversations to be free enough to flow, naturally bringing Jesus into those topics or discussions.

Where Do I Find It?

Boldness, Confidence: 9, 31, 34
Joshua 1:9; Job 42:1–2; Jeremiah 20:9; Matthew 16:18–19, 17:20, 25:14–30; Mark 16:15; John 14:12, 17:16, 18, 21:15–17; Acts 1:8, 4:13; Romans 10:14–15; Ephesians 1:11–12, 19–20; Philippians 1:6, 4:13; Colossians 1:28–29, 4:5–7; 1 John 3:18

Broken Hearts: 10, 15, 20
Genesis 6:5–6; Psalm 30:2–3, 11–12, 27:10, 34:17–18, 68:5, 73:25–26, 147:3; Isaiah 53:3; Jeremiah 31:13; Luke 7:12–14; Romans 8:18–30; 1 Corinthians 13:4–8; Revelation 21:4

Broken Trust: 7
Isaiah 26:3; Psalm 28:7; Matthew 11:28; Matthew 26:47–56; Romans 12:21; 2 Timothy 2:13

Depression: 57
Job 19:25–27; Psalm 23, 71:5; Isaiah 60:1–2; Isaiah 61:1–3; Lamentations 3:21–24; Matthew 18:20; John 11:25; John 16:33; 1 Peter 1:3

Envy: 56
Genesis 4:3–7; Proverbs 14:30; 1 Corinthians 13:4; Galatians 5:19–21; 1 Timothy 6:3–7; James 3:14–16, 4:1–3

Encouragement: 11, 51
Psalm 42, 73:25–26, 138:3, 7–8; Proverbs 13:12; Ecclesiastes 4:9–12; Isaiah 43:2, 51:12; Jeremiah 29:11–14; Lamentations 3; Philippians 2:1–4; Hebrews 6:17–18

Enemy's Schemes, The: 33
Psalm 143:3–4; John 8:44, 10:10; Acts 10:38; 2 Corinthians 2:11, 11:14; 1 John 3:8; 1 Peter 5:8–9; Revelation 12:17

Eternal Life, Salvation: 13, 45
Deuteronomy 31:8; Psalm 27:1; Isaiah 59:17, 61:10; Romans 5:1–2, 8:15; 2 Corinthians 6:17–18; Ephesians 1:3–14, 6:13, 17; Colossians 1:15–20, 3:1–4; 1 Thessalonians 5:8; 1 Peter 1:3

Faith: 44
Psalm 18, 28:7; Proverbs 18:10; Isaiah 42:3; Romans 8:31–39; 1 Corinthians 10:13; Ephesians 2:8–9, 6:13, 16; 1 Thessalonians 5:8; Hebrews 11; 1 Peter 5:8–9; 1 John 5:4–5

Fear, Fear of Death: 12, 25, 30
Deuteronomy 3:21–22; Psalm 40:3–4, 56:3, 118:5–7, 139:14–16;
Isaiah 43:1–3; Matthew 10:26–28; Luke 9:24; John 3:16, 14:1–6;
1 Corinthians 15:12–23; Philippians 1:21–24, 3:10, 4:6–7; 1 John 4:18

Friendship: 28, 50
1 Samuel 16:7, 20:42; 2 Samuel 1:23; Job 2:11–13, 13:4–5; Proverbs
13:20, 17:17, 17:27–28; Ecclesiastes 4:9–12; John 15:12–15; 2 Corinthians 1:4; Philippians 2:1–11

God's Love: 14, 53
Genesis 1:27; Zephaniah 3:17; Psalm 18:19, 139:13; John 15:13–16;
Romans 8:31–35; 2 Corinthians 2:14; Ephesians 1:11–12, 2:4–6

Guilt and Shame: 2
Psalm 103:12; Acts 13:38–39; Romans 4:7–8, 5:16–19, 8:1–4,
33–39; 2 Corinthians 7:9–10; Jude v. 24

Hard Times: 26
Psalm 126:4–6; Jeremiah 29:11–14; John 14:27; 2 Corinthians 4:7–9

Heaven, Hell: 24, 60
Matthew 7:13–14; Mark 9:43–48; Luke 10:20; John 14:2–3, 15:11;
Romans 14:7; 2 Corinthians 5:6–10; 1 Thessalonians 1:5–10; Hebrews
11:13–16; James 1:17; 1 Peter 1:8

Heart Matters, Your Heart: 29, 38
Psalm 51:10, 61:2; Proverbs 4:23; Matthew 12:33–35, 15:18–19;
Mark 12:30–33; John 8:3–11; Romans 10:9–10; Ephesians 1:18–19

Holy Spirit: 39
1 Kings 19:11–12; Matthew 10:19–20; Acts 1:8, 8:29–31, 8:35–40,
13:2–3, 16:6–10, 18:9–11, 20:22

Identity, Self-Image: 3, 17, 36
Job 31:13–14; Daniel 3:16–18; Matthew 7:4–5; John 10:7–15;
Romans 12:1–2; 1 Corinthians 9:22–23; 2 Corinthians 5:17; Philippians
3:4–9; Galatians 2:20, 6:14; Ephesians 5:8; 1 Thessalonians 2:8;
1 Peter 2:9; 1 John 1:8–9; 1 John 5:20

Jealousy: 55
Genesis 4:3–7; Proverbs 14:30; 1 Corinthians 13:4; 1 Timothy 6:3–5;
James 1:17, 3:14–16

Life in Christ: 5
John 15:1–11; Romans 8:11; Galatians 2:20; James 2:17; 1 John 2:24–28

Loneliness: 1
Deuteronomy 31:6–8; Joshua 1:5; Psalm 23:4; Mark 15:33–39; John 14:16–19, 16:4–15; Colossians 1:27

Loss: 32
2 Samuel 22:32–34; Psalm 61:1–4, 62:1–2; Matthew 27:45–46; Mark 15:34; Acts 14:21–23; 2 Corinthians 12:9

Lust: 27
Job 31:1; Proverbs 6:20–29; John 14:6; Romans 6–7, 8:5; 1 Thessalonians 4:3–8; James 1:14–15; 1 Peter 2:11

Love, Loving Others: 22, 37
Matthew 5:46–48; John 13:34–35, 15:9, 12; 1 Corinthians 13:13; Ephesians 5:1–2; 1 Thessalonians 3:12–13; 1 John 3:18, 4:10–12

Making Jesus Contagious: 54
Matthew 5:15–16; Luke 19:2–10; John 13:35

Materialism, Contentment: 8, 18
Deuteronomy 4:24; 1 Kings 3:5–14; Proverbs 15:16; Ecclesiastes 5:10–12; Matthew 6:19–34; Luke 12:15–21; 2 Corinthians 8:9; Philippians 4:11–13; 1 Timothy 6:6–10

Past Mistakes, Regret, Failure: 49, 52, 58
Psalm 103:10–14; Ezekiel 36:26–27; Mark 14:43–46; John 21:15–19; Acts 22:1–21; Romans 3:23, 25, 5:8, 8:1–11, 12:1–2; 2 Corinthians 1:3–4, 5:17, 12:9–10; Ephesians 2:8–10; Philippians 3:13; Hebrews 12:1–2; 1 John 1:7

Peace: 43
Isaiah 52:7; Ephesians 2:14, 6:15; 2 Timothy 2:22; 1 Peter 3:8–12

Peer Pressure: 19
Matthew 26:69–75; John 18:25–27; Romans 1:16; 2 Timothy 1:8; 1 John 4:18

Prayer: 48
Luke 18:1–7; Romans 8:26–27; Galatians 4:6; Philippians 4:6–7; 1 Thessalonians 5:17; Jude v. 20

Righteousness: 16, 42

Genesis 1:27; Genesis 15:6; Psalm 18:20, 24; Isaiah 11:5, 59:17, 61:10 – 11; Matthew 5:13 – 14; Romans 3:21 – 26, 10:3 – 4; 1 Corinthians 1:30 – 31; 2 Corinthians 5:17 – 21; Ephesians 6:13 – 14; Philippians 3:9; Hebrews 10:14

Sharing Faith: 23

1 Corinthians 2:1 – 5; 2 Corinthians 2:16, 5:20; Ephesians 6:19

Serving Others: 40

Mark 10:45; John 17:9 – 23; Galatians 6:9; Philippians 2:2 – 8; 1 Peter 4:10

Sexual Boundaries: 59

Psalm 119:9; Song of Solomon 8:4; John 10:10; 1 Corinthians 6:18 – 20; Ephesians 5:1 – 20; Hebrews 13:4

Sword of the Spirit: 46

Psalm 119:11; Isaiah 40:8; Luke 4:1 – 12; John 1:14; Ephesians 6:13, 17; Hebrews 4:12 – 13; Revelation 1:16; Revelation 12:11; Revelation 19:15

Trusting God: 47

2 Kings 18:5; Psalm 31:13 – 15; Proverbs 3:5 – 6; Daniel 3:28; Colossians 2:7 – 10

Truth: 41

Psalm 25:4 – 5; Isaiah 11:5; John 3:21, 14:6; Ephesians 4:15, 25, 6:14; 2 Peter 2:1 – 3; 1 John 1:5 – 10; 1 John 4:6; 3 John 1:3 – 4

Weakness, Brokenness: 21, 35

Joshua 2, 6:17; Matthew 5:3 – 10, 9:11 – 13; Romans 7:15, 19 – 20; 1 Corinthians 1:27; 2 Corinthians 1:4, 12:9; James 2:25; 1 John 4:10 – 11

Wholeness: 4

Matthew 19:20 – 21; John 10:10; Philippians 1:6, 3:8 – 10; Hebrews 2:10; James 1:4

Worry: 6

Exodus 16:16 – 21; Matthew 6:25 – 34; Mark 4:35 – 41; Philippians 4:6 – 7

Youth For Christ Programs

With a passion to reach every young person, one at a time, Youth For Christ/USA® (**www.yfc.org**) has been operating local ministry centers across the country since 1944. Today's most widely practiced programs include Campus Life®, City Life®, Deaf Teen Quest, Teen Parents®, and Juvenile Justice Ministries®. YFC/USA is also one of over 100 fully charted nations, participating in the international movement of Youth For Christ, providing opportunities to serve around the world through Project Serve® (**www. projectserve.org**) and World Outreach (**www.yfcworldoutreach. org**). For more information about 3Story®, visit **www.3story.org**.

City Life®

YFC's City Life helps young people in urban communities through teaching life skills, building relationships with caring adult role models, providing opportunities for positive peer group experiences, and sharing the good news of the gospel of Jesus Christ.

Teen Parents®

YFC's Teen Parents connects trained adults with pregnant girls and teenage parents in programs designed to help them make good choices and establish a solid foundation in Christ, not only in their lives, but also in the lives of their babies.

Juvenile Justice Ministries®

YFC's Juvenile Justice Ministries reaches troubled young people through juvenile justice and social service agency contacts. Juvenile Justice Ministries connects them with trained adults who help them make good choices and find healing and new life in Christ.

Campus Life®

YFC's Campus Life combines healthy relationships with creative programs to help middle school and senior high young people make good choices, establish a solid foundation for life, and positively impact their schools for Christ. Campus Life is a place to make friends, talk about everyday life, and discover the beginning of a life–long relationship with Jesus Christ.

Deaf Teen Quest®

YFC Deaf Teen Quest is a part of the Campus Life outreach that is designed specifically to build life-changing relationships with deaf and hard of hearing students. Teams of caring Christian adults enter the world of deaf teenagers with "fun, friendship, fellowship, and faith." YFC Deaf Teen Quest provides a healthy peer group environment with Christian role models to help deaf teens develop a mature faith that makes a positive difference in the world.

YFCAMP® (yfc.org/camp)

YFC's YFCAMP exists to create an outdoor environment that invites God to transform the lives of young people through shared experiences, outdoor challenges, and times of solitude. Additionally, local YFC ministry centers host numerous camps around the nation.

World Outreach

YFC/USA's World Outreach serves YFC International, sending missionaries to serve as an integral part of indigenous YFC ministries in nations spanning the globe from Bolivia to New Zealand.

Project Serve®

For three decades, YFC's Project Serve has sent thousands of young people and adults on mission trips in partnership with over 90 indigenous YFC ministries.

YFCM/Club Beyond (yfc.org/military)

YFC's Military Youth Ministry equips ministry centers in the USA with resources and training to reach military youth in their community. And, in partnership with Military Community Youth Ministries, YFCM places youth workers on military bases around the world.

Talk It Up!

Want free books?
First looks at the best new fiction?
Awesome exclusive merchandise?

We want to hear from you!

Give us your opinions on titles, covers, and stories.
Join the Z Street Team.

Visit zstreetteam.zondervan.com/joinnow
to sign up today!

Also—Friend us on Facebook!

www.facebook.com/goodteenreads

- Video Trailers
- Connect with your favorite authors
- Sneak peeks at new releases
- Giveaways
- Fun discussions
- And much more!